Places Where I've Done Time

Places make us — let's not imagine that once were here anything else does. First genes, then places — after that it's every man for himself, God help us, and good luck to one and all.

The fascinating thing most likely though is how the same place — a miserable school, for instance, with rotten teachers — bores one man into art, and drives another into crime — the only two arenas we really have: art, making: crime, taking. (The genes, the genes, cries the man who believes inheritance, not environment, does it. But does it? Alone? I have never seen poor people in the slums who were not equal to being instantly clean and refined in a mansion with a million dollars. And take away the millionaire's money and put him in the slums and how elegant will he be fighting mice and cockroaches?

Yes all well and good perhaps you are saying, but doesn't that mean that people make us? Of course, but people are places.

William Saroyan describes what "Places" mean to him.

Places
Where I've Done Time

William Saroyan

PRAEGER PUBLISHERS

New York • Washington

BOOKS THAT MATTER

Published in the United States of America in 1972
by Praeger Publishers, Inc.
111 Fourth Avenue, New York, N. Y. 10003

Library of Congress Catalog Card Number: 70–178227

Printed in the United States of America

This book is for Armenians, half Armenians, quarter Armenians, and one-eighth Armenians.

Sixteenth and thirty-second Armenians, and other winners, are likelier to be happy with a useful book.

Places Where I've Done Time

With illustrations by the author

Places Where I've Done Time

1. Tanforan Race Track, San Francisco, 1932

AT TANFORAN I USED TO FEEL GREAT. WHY DID A LITTLE San Francisco race track affect me that way?

Well, some places are happy places and some aren't, and that's pretty much all you can say about the matter. But if you think on it, you soon discover that no place is *totally* without happiness, possibly not even the grave —but we're not going there, you and I. When we die, it just isn't going to be us. Coming around the stretch, boxed in, we're going to find a little opening, and before anybody knows what's going on, we're going to ease through, and move out, and come down to the wire all alone, and go away, hollering and laughing, uncaught again, again uncatchable.

I had no money, and so it wasn't often I could go. Now and then somebody driving south would give me a lift. Before taking off I'd borrow a couple of dollars from my brother Henry, or I'd take the money I'd set aside for an emergency. Near the entrance gate I'd ask where I might get a pass. Somebody would tell me to try John Dabb at the gas station across the road, or somebody would come along with an extra pass, so I'd get in free. Half a dollar saved right there.

Soon enough I'd see somebody I knew.

"Today's the day," Archie Minasian would shout from fifty yards away. "A winner in every race. Money galore." People would look around and half-smile or half-scowl.

We would count our money, study the entries, and make temporary decisions, knowing we'd change them later on. We would walk back and forth, smoking cigarettes and shouting at each other. I was twenty-four and he was nineteen, my mother's kid sister's son.

One Saturday Archie's money was eighty cents, mine was a dollar sixty. Thus, we had enough for only one two-dollar bet.

We laughed at the problem, and had a cup of coffee apiece, to think it over.

"Well, now," I said, "with this coffee and a fresh pack of cigarettes apiece, we've got exactly two dollars between us, and these three pennies."

"Throw the pennies away for good luck," Archie said. And, seeing that I made no move to do so, he struck the bottom of my open hand and sent the pennies flying.

"You damn fool," I shouted. "One of those pennies might have been a 1918 Lincoln S."

"What do you mean?"

"Always look at your pennies before you throw them away. A 1918 Lincoln S is worth eleven thousand dollars."

"Jesus, I can use that money," Archie said. We hurried to where the pennies had fallen and began to look for them.

"We've still got our two dollars," I said. "Shall we bet the first race, or wait?"

"Better wait," Archie said.

A long shot won the race, and Archie said, "If we'd had him, we'd be collecting forty-eight dollars and forty cents right now. I *liked* Grisby. I liked Grisby first thing this morning, when I saw he was running."

We laughed and went back where the pennies had fallen and looked for them again, but again without any luck.

"I could use a hot dog," I said, and Archie said, "Throw away a dime? Break into our gambling money? Well, get me one, too, then, it's early, something will happen."

We had a hot dog apiece, a cup of coffee apiece, and nothing in the world ever tasted so good. The horses we picked but didn't bet ran out of the money, so we felt we were entitled to good things to eat and drink.

And the lighting up of new cigarettes made us enterprising and practical.

"How much have we got *now*?" Archie asked when the horses came on the track for the fourth race.

"A dollar forty."

"Sixty cents short. If I had a lot of money, I'd bet a chunk on Hackensack."

"He's thirty to one."

"After the race, I'd be rich."

"I hope he wins. Number 11. Well, let's watch him. His colors are all red."

"Just my luck, not to have a pot of money on a sure winner," Archie said. "I wish we had back the sixty cents we wasted on food, so we could bet Hackensack two dollars, at least."

It was a good start. All twelve horses got away at approximately the same time—excepting Hackensack, who seemed to get the idea that it was a race or something like a race only after he'd seen all of the other horses going away.

Archie said, "Look at him go."

"I *am* looking." He was last by twelve lengths before the first turn.

"Watch him trample them to death," Archie said.

The race was over when Hackensack leveled off into the stretch and came pounding home.

"Look at him go," Archie said.

"Good thing you didn't have a lot of money on him."

"How much have we got *now*?" Archie said.

"Still a dollar forty."

"I would have sworn I lost money on that race. Shall we have a hamburger?"

We had a hamburger and another cup of coffee apiece. We went back to where the pennies had fallen, but again we didn't find them. We just laughed about having thrown them away.

"It's no laughing matter," Archie said. "Eleven thousand dollars isn't something to throw away."

And so it went. The weather was good. It was better at Tanforan than in San Francisco, only eight miles away. There was a nice smell at Tanforan—of earth, horses, people, money, hot dogs, hamburgers, coffee, cigarette smoke, and something else. I really don't know what the other thing was. Was it comedy hovering over and crowding around everybody?

2. Joaquin Miller's Hillside Cottage in Oakland, 1912

ONE DAY HENRY WAS TAKEN WITH TWO DOZEN OTHER boys to the hillside home of Joaquin Miller, who wrote a poem called *Columbus,* which to this day appears in many American school books.

"Wahkeen Miller," Henry said. "That's who we saw."

"Why didn't they take me?" I said.

"Only for big boys," Henry said. "He's very old, has a long beard, lies on a couch, doesn't want to see little boys. He spoke to us."

"What did he say?"

" 'Now, boys, I've planted a thousand eucalyptus trees all over these Oakland hills, and I want you boys to plant trees wherever you go, too."

"What else?"

" 'What's your name,' and Melvin Athey said, 'Melvin Athey,' and then he said, 'And you, what's your name,' and I said, 'Henry Saroyan.' "

"If he asked me, I would have said, 'Puddin tame, ask me again, I'll tell you the same.' "

"Ah, you don't say that when Wahkeen Miller asks you. He's an old man."

I never met Joaquin Miller, but whenever I remember the small boys (who believed they were the big boys) standing at attention in his hillside cottage, I smile and feel good. The man was such a nice phoney. "And *you,*

17

what's *your* name? "Benediction. And my brother Henry
told him. He came right out and said his name to the
old fraud, whose own name was *not* Joaquin. It was
Cincinnatus Hiner. He changed Cincinnatus Hiner to
Joaquin because he thought it sounded better with
Miller.

3. 2378 Sutter Street at Divisadero, San Francisco, 1929

WHEN I CAME BACK FROM NEW YORK IN JANUARY OF the year 1929, I was in no mood to take anything seriously, for I considered my four months in New York a total failure, and my return to the large long unfurnished flat on the third floor at 2378 Sutter Street in San Francisco an event of embarrassment, for I had set out in late August of 1928 by Greyhound bus in the expectation of never going back to the comfortable, purposeless, quarrelsome, impossible life at home.

But there I was, in my 21st year, with my big, proud ideas eaten like an old hat, and there was the rest of the small family, apparently glad to see me. I shared the back room with my brother. I had my own desk, like a man in business, only now I was out of business.

But just getting back and seeing everybody, and then going to the back room and seeing my bed all neatly made, and my desk all dusted and everything on top of it in order, made me feel great. I sat at my desk and reflected on the enormity of my failure in New York, and I felt glad to be out of a crazy expectation like that—to become a great writer—no, a great man, but not so much to *become* a great man as to make known to the world at large that I *was* a great man. I felt glad that I didn't have to keep trying to decide what to write in order most effectively and speedily to bring about that condition.

I got up from the desk and looked out the window at the back end of Mount Zion Hospital, across the street on Sutter, and far down Sutter to Fillmore, and I thought, "Now, all I've got to do is find a job, take out one of the nurses across the street, marry her, and settle down, that's all. Nothing but fun."

Lying on top of his bed, Henry said, "What's the matter?"

"What do you mean?"

"Why aren't you writing?"

"Henry, man does not live by writing alone."

He sat up. "What kind of bullshit is that?"

"Come on," I said, "let's walk down to Fillmore, and then on to the Public Library."

We hurried down the three flights of stairs and out to the street, laughing as if we had just heard a great joke, and then we began to run.

But when we stopped, Henry said, "Christ. Tomorrow's Monday. Well, you better find a job. Get up at six when I get up, and go to the employment agencies. It's great at six."

"I know," I said. "I've been getting up at four in New York. I know how great it is early in the morning."

4. The Opera Club, 24 Avenue de l' Opéra, Paris, 1949

YESTERDAY, AS THE MONTH OF JULY, 1969, APPROACHED its end forever, around four in the afternoon, I left 74 Rue Taitbout and began to walk—for a little change of scene, a little exercise, and for the good of my soul. At the Place d'Estienne d'Orves I went up the ramp to Trinité, where a hearse was in the driveway, loaded with flowers, and three uniformed funeral parlor workers stood chatting and waiting for the services inside to be concluded, so they could proceed with their work.

I went in and watched the people up front, and the priest on the platform mumbling Latin, squatting and getting up, while a boy in a proper robe stood by, waiting his turn to do something.

I then went around the corner on Clichy to the bargain box outside the little bookstore where for eight years I have been paying a dime apiece for books in English—the best bargains in town. But this time I didn't feel like buying another three or four. I felt like walking, so I went up Londres, down Amsterdam past Gare St. Lazare, a very famous railway station in poem, song, story, and drama, and from there down to the Boulevard—Capucine, and the Café de la Paix, where the same people were sitting at the outside tables that

I seemed to have seen the first time I walked past that place, in 1935.

And I saw the place again in June of the year 1949, twenty years ago—damned if I know how all that time went away the way it did, unnoticed—I had just come up to Paris from Lisbon by way of Biarritz, and I was short of money. I was stopping at the Scribe, forty-one years old. What to do? What to do? It was all slow, it was all stupid, everything was wrong. Perhaps I ought to have a couple of drinks and do a little gambling.

There was a young cop directing traffic in the middle of the square, so I went to him and said in English, "Is there a gambling house around here somewhere?"

A joke, I thought. I believed he wouldn't understand, or would say no, gambling is against the law in Paris. Instead, he pointed across the square to a building. I noticed that along the third floor was the word BATA spelled out in big neon letters. Was that perhaps the name of the gambling house?

No, it was the Opera Club, on the third floor. BATA was on the floor above, whatever BATA was and is.

The house was dealing baccarat, so I tossed French paper on the green table. In an hour I won better than a couple of hundred dollars, so I walked back to the hotel and had a shower.

My cousin Chesley Saroyan came up, a man I had known from the time of his birth in Fresno, not yet thirty years old. We talked and went out to walk, and he asked me to go to dinner with him and his wife.

Great, I said. We went back to the Opera Club and I tossed a hundred dollars on the green table and lost, and another hundred and lost, and then it was serious, because all I had left in the world was two hundred, but I tossed it all on the table and won, and put my own two hundred back in my pocket and let the other two hundred ride, and won, so now I had a nice profit of four hundred dollars for the day.

My cousin thought I was crazy. We had a good evening.

5. The Santa Fe Depot, Fresno, 1922

THE SOUTHERN PACIFIC DEPOT ON TULARE BETWEEN H and G streets was a place of endless fascination, and so was the Santa Fe Depot, also on Tulare Street but at the other side of town. The trains moved slowly through the residential sections of both sides of town, whistles hooting and bells tolling slowly.

One year on my way home after work at the Postal Telegraph Office, around half past twelve at night, I remember arriving at the Santa Fe Depot just as a very long passenger train from San Francisco stopped and passengers began to get off.

About two dozen members of a family were standing on the siding waiting for somebody. They were the Arakelians—Krikor, his wife, his sons, his daughters, and other members of the family.

At last his son, Eddie, about twenty-four, got off the train, and everybody began to make happy sounds of speech and laughter, while Eddie himself hugged his mother and then his father and then one by one everybody else there. If a total stranger had been there, Eddie would have hugged him, too.

I watched it all. Krikor Arakelian was the Wine King of California and a millionaire. He came to the First Armenian Presbyterian Church, so I knew him, but now at the depot I stayed out of sight, watching and waiting for the long train to pull away, so I could continue my ride home, to 3204 El Monte Way.

All of the Arakelians laughed, roly-poly Eddie laughed, and I laughed.

He had been in New York the whole year managing his father's winery and office in lower Manhattan, but now he'd come home by train for Christmas—and the world was wonderful. Three thousand miles was nothing, you got on a train, you had your own private little room, you changed at Chicago, you ate great meals in the diner, you read mystery stories and newspapers in the club car, and then all of a sudden there you were back in Fresno, and there everybody was, standing on the station platform waiting for you. Who could ask for anything more?

Four months ago I went to the Sante Fe Depot in Fresno at eleven at night to catch the train to Chicago and New York, and I remembered exactly where Eddie had got off and where his whole family had stood, waiting for him. It made me laugh with happiness all over again.

6. 1881 Broadway, San Francisco, 1938

QUITE A FEW WRITERS, DOWN THE AGES, AND DOWN THE backstreets and alleys of the world, have given detailed accounts of their astonishing achievements with women, but inasmuch as I have found such writing impossible to read, I will only remark that there was this woman I enjoyed sleeping with in her apartment in San Francisco. And then I will go about my business, which is simply to remember places in which a sense of reality came to me that impelled me to feel great.

This apartment was such a place. It was beautifully furnished, and it had a grand view of the Golden Gate. It smelled good, and it smelled of the woman herself, who, altogether without perfume upon her, had a scent that was delicious to breathe, especially after a night of roaring about town in saloons. There was booze there, in a whole small bar cart, and sparkling glasses and sparkling ice.

And it seemed that no matter when I phoned the woman said, "Come on up, the door's unlatched. If I'm asleep help yourself."

And so, going in, I'd look down the hill at the Golden Gate, fix a big drink, take a big swallow, light a cigarette, inhale, and go into the next room for a look at the woman—large, well-made, honest, and smelling like all the rest of the truth of the human race in the world:

that part of the truth that just isn't in anything other than a handsome and honest woman. That was it, that was what everything was about—that scent of the rest of the truth, the completion of it, which was in the body and hair and nature of women. You could get to a lot of truth without it, of course, but it wouldn't be complete, it couldn't be.

7. The YMCA at 23rd Street and 7th Avenue, New York, 1928

THE YOUNG MEN'S CHRISTIAN ASSOCIATION IN FRESNO was on Broadway above the Public Library. It was a place both ridiculed and exploited. One Saturday morning in 1922 there was an unforgettable illustrated talk on venereal diseases, followed by a free visit to the gym and pool, and that was enough for me.

When the Greyhound bus finally arrived in New York, and I got off, to make my way to fame and fortune late in August, 1928, the hour was almost midnight, everything was closed, I had been traveling for ten days, I was excited, tired, angry, and I didn't know what to do or where to go. I knew nobody. I had no letter of introduction to anybody. Cash on hand came to a dollar and a few coins. The rest of my money, almost a hundred dollars, was in my suitcase, and the suitcase was lost, stolen, or misdirected—that's what the baggage clerk in New York said. It would be tracked down, he said. The number of the baggage check was written down, and I went out into the midnight streets of New York.

First I ran two New York blocks. Maybe it was from having sat so long. Maybe it was from having no money. Maybe it was from feeling lousy. But the running stopped that, and made me feel good. I was light. And I had no luggage. I didn't know where I was going, but I was going swiftly. At each corner I looked to see what was around. At 23rd Street I saw the big YMCA sign in lights. I said to myself, "That's it. I'll go there."

The room was a dollar in advance, and that left very little, but even a little is something. The cafeteria was closed, but the clerk said if I hurried back the man might make me a sandwich. He made a big one—ham and cheese both—and he took only a dime instead of fifteen cents, because it had been his idea to throw in the ham. I took the sandwich up to the room, and saw a bed, a wash basin, and a drinking glass. I ran the water out of the tap until it was cool, filled the glass, sat down at the rickety desk, and began to eat the sandwich and drink the cold water. I drank four glasses of the cold water before I finished the sandwich—it was so good I kept saying to myself, "I'll make it, lost suitcase or not. I'll make it."

There was a shower down the hall, so I went there and had a great shower and walked back to the room and got in bed and went to sleep.

8. Postal Telegraph Office, 651 Market Street, San Francisco, 1927

I WAS COUNTER CLERK AT THE SMALL BRANCH OFFICE of the Postal Telegraph Company at 651 Market Street in San Francisco, in the famous Palace Hotel Building, in the month of September, 1927. San Francisco was in my blood and bones. I knew it as a very small child and a little later as a whistling boy standing outside the building on Laguna Street in which my mother had a furnished room, waiting for her to come home from her day's work somewhere. And still later at the Panama-Pacific International Exposition, or the World's Fair, of 1915.

I went to a little school on McAllister Street near Franklin, but not for long. The Orphanage people felt that it wasn't right for me to be so much on my own, and so one day my mother packed a picnic, we took the ferry and crossed the Bay, and then a streetcar, and pretty soon we were back at Fred Finch, where a favorite song was "There is an orphanage far, far away, where they have pork and beans every Saturday. Oh, how the children yell when they hear the dinner bell. Oh, how the children yell far, far away."

The rest of the family was sent for by special messengers from the Superintendent's office—and they soon arrived: Cosette, 14, Zabe, 11, and Henry, 8. We took the picnic to the hillside and spread a blanket and sat and ate and talked.

Far below was San Francisco across the Bay. I had been there. I knew its streets.

And now, fourteen years later, I was working on Market Street. A man came into the office, sat at one of the three tables, and for about an hour he wrote a telegram and crumpled it and threw it in the wastepaper basket, and then at last he came to the counter, and I counted the words in the telegram, looked at him, told him the charge, and he went away. Mr. Lincoln Steffens, with a neat little mustache and a neat little Van Dyke beard.

Years later I read around in his autobiography and liked it very much, and remembered (by God) having met the man. It hadn't really been a meeting, but it had been better than nothing. He was a stocky little man, with pince-nez glasses attached to the top of the bridge of his nose. He seemed hot and very excited, or, as the old American expression used to have it, nervous.

Are newspapermen, are writers, novelists, historians, humorists, are they all hot, excited, and nervous? In books about Mark Twain that I have accumulated over the years, several of the people who worked in his home put it quite plainly—he was always in a state, he was always keyed up, he was always nervous, and frequently a nervous wreck.

Make allowances for the writers being household managers, or secretaries, and not especially accurate in their observing and writing, it is still necessary to think about what they have said. From his writing, and from his image, as it is called by Madison Avenue, and from his lectures, one does not get the impression that Mark

Twain was a jittery character. On the contrary, he was calm, cool, and collected, drawing in on his fine cigar, or merely brandishing it for emphasis. But that may have been the performance: that may have been the *consequence* of all of the nervousness.

My mother's kid brother, when he was 70 and I was almost 55, was asked by students at a Persian university to tell them something about his nephew the writer, and this is what he said: "Willie was nervous." I read it in English in a newspaper clipping and roared with laughter.

But then I thought, "Is that all that came through to the man?"

Well, apparently it was. If Lincoln Steffens was nervous in 1927, aged 40, he wasn't half as nervous as I was, aged 19—and not about the wording of a telegram, but about everything.

9. Emerson School Playground, L and San Benito, Fresno, 1918

I HATED SCHOOL, EVEN WHEN I DID NOTHING BUT HAVE fun all day.

I was as paranoid then as I am now, so I saw a lot of monkey business going on behind the scenes involving me.

I didn't want to fail a semester, because that meant staying back, and if anything filled my heart with terror it was the condition of not moving on.

At least once a week one or another of the teachers let me know that I was failing, and it looked as if I'd be kept back.

The rest of the class would be promoted, but I would remain in the same class and be surrounded by a lot of new little kids.

This scared me, but it also made me fight back— by ridiculing the school, the principal, the teachers, the subjects, and the students (all of whom were going to be promoted while I was going to be left back).

There wasn't a course in which I didn't excel, so what was the plotting about?

It was about *this:* I was so bored that I made remarks all day long. (Well, sometimes I didn't. I sometimes fell to dreaming, and kept my mouth shut all day. Or I became both bored and depressed and didn't want any part of the action, at all.)

During the ten-minute recess morning and afternoon, I would race out to the playground and ask myself, "Lord, Lord, what are we to do, what are we to do? It is all so stupid, so boring, so everlastingly slow."

Al Nidevar would take a stance and begin to recite his version of *Hiawatha*—as if in answer to the groaning of my spirit and the desperation of my soul. He was an Irish boy, the kid brother of Mark Nidevar. They lived with their mother Mary on South Van Ness past the California Playground, near the Southern Pacific tracks. Al Nidevar was the greatest imitator of Henry Wadsworth Longfellow's crazy Indians in the whole world, and he knew he could count on me to appreciate his astonishing virtuosity in exposing the emptiness of that monotonous and repetitious saga. Al Nidevar saved many a day for me at Emerson School.

He helped me with my paranoia. I never was kept back, but the teachers were always saying that I would be.

10. The First Methodist Church, Oakland, 1913

DUCK EGGS FOR SUNDAY BREAKFAST, BECAUSE SUNDAY WAS different, special, holy, God's day, man's day, child's day. Boiled duck eggs. One apiece, and an extra egg for any boy at the table who got there first. I tended to. The duck egg is a good bit larger than the egg of the hen. It seemed to have a slightly deeper flavor too, richer, more satisfying. All egg yolks in those days *were* yolks, were real, were golden yellow, not faded yellow, and the yolk of a duck egg was really something to get to and have. And, because the day was Sunday and God's, there was almost always something else extra, a kind of last-minute surprise, although everybody came to expect it. Somebody would get up and say, "A special treat this Sunday morning are fresh strawberries, donated by Mr. and Mrs. Clarence Converse of Alameda." Cheers, and immediately bowls of strawberries would be brought to every table and everybody would reach out and take his bowl. Duck eggs, and strawberries, too.

After breakfast everybody checked everybody else, lined up, and at a signal began to walk to the First Methodist Church, six blocks away, like the Christian soldiers of the hymn. I never liked being put into the ranks, and I tried to get a place in the last row of four, so I could fall back and not feel I was hemmed in. All the same, when I was sick one Sunday morning, and the church bells tolled, and the smell of apple blossoms came up to the attic room I occupied alone, having an illness that might be contagious, and a fever that wore out my soul, and I heard the boys after breakfast, and from the window saw my group fall in and march off, I wished I were with them.

Once we arrived at the church, it wasn't anywhere near as bad as we liked to complain on the way. In any case, we had our own escape hatches. We managed to find comedy in being there. We asked for songs to which we had words of our own, which we considered more appropriate and certainly more interesting.

> At the bar, at the bar
> where I smoked my last cigar
> and the nickels and the dimes
> rolled away
>
> it was there by chance
> I tore my Sunday pants

Alas, time has worn away the last two lines, but not the memory of their power to enchant and delight us.

But it was during the minister's long prayer that my mind was most deeply illuminated by comedy. As he said his incredible words, I saw actions involving himself and other people I knew, and these actions were very entertaining. Furthermore, the visions and actions came directly from his words and his voice and manner of speech, which was pleading and whiney.

11. Captain Heath's Office, Steamer's Division, the Southern Pacific, Embarcadero and Mission Street, San Francisco, 1926

IN 1926 I WENT TO SONORA, CALIFORNIA FROM FRESNO by train to take a job at the U.S. Forestry Service, didn't like the set-up, left a message, and took a bus to San Francisco, where I applied for a job at the Southern Pacific, at 65 Market Street. They sent me to Captain Heath in the Steamer's Division at the foot of Mission Street on the Embarcadero, second floor.

He was a big man who had retired as an ocean-going captain and had accepted this easy job on the waterfront, managing the passenger ferry boats plying back and forth between San Francisco and Oakland, and the river boats that went up the deltas and branches of the Sacramento and San Joaquin rivers to Stockton and Sacramento.

Our interview was brief. He said, "I want a boy who can type, do a little bookkeeping, and run a lot of errands quickly."

"Yes, sir," I said, because that is the thing to say when a life-saving and interesting job is at stake.

"All right," Captain Heath said. "You're hired, as of this morning. I'm throwing in the five hours. Go on up to the sixth floor at 65 Market and let the Doctor give you a clearance. It's routine."

"Yes, sir."

The Doctor was an old sour-souled man who nevertheless was not stupid or mean. He used the hammer at the knee, ran a nail down the flesh of the torso, right and left, noticed the quivering reflex, scribbled something on a mimeographed form, signed it, folded it, and said, "Give that to Captain Heath."

I have always believed in asking a question if the answer might prove interesting and is given free of charge.

"Is anything wrong?" I said.

The old Doctor looked at me, didn't smile, and then said in a mumble with just a trace of laughter in it, "You'll live," and then added even more softly, "Forever, most likely."

I worked with Captain Heath's two dozen other slaves for eight or nine days, men and women, and it was kind of great, but I took to the work with so much enthusiasm that there was noise and humming and whistling and singing in my going and coming, and I kept my cap on my head, in order not to be slowed down.

"Hang your cap up when you come in," Captain Heath said one day.

"Yes, sir," I said, but came in an hour later and didn't hang it up. He said his piece again, and I said mine, and it happened the next day again, so I hung up my cap, sat down at a typewriter, wrote a resignation that I felt Zola would have been proud of, took it straight to Captain Heath and handed it to him: he read it, looked at me, couldn't figure something out, had my wages tallied, and paid me. (I was bored, and I wanted to take a boat and go somewhere, that's all it really was.)

12. The White Fawn Saloon, Mariposa Street, Fresno, 1916

THE TEMPLE BAR BUILDING WAS ON THE SOUTHWEST corner of Van Ness and Mariposa. I had no idea that it had any connection with anything other than itself. I liked the name, but I didn't know anything about its derivation. Alas, to this day I don't, although I know the building in Fresno bore the same name as a rather famous building in London. The owners of the building were not Armenians, they were English. They were different, but not much different. The really different people were the Chinese of Chinatown, across the Southern Pacific tracks. They looked different, and had a very special way of using their voices in speech. There was singing in their talk, and they stood and walked in a way that nobody else did—not even their neighbors the Japanese and the Sikhs of India, both of whom worked in the vineyards.

Down from the Temple Bar Building, across the street on Mariposa, was the White Fawn Saloon, with a long bar, free lunch, tables, and in the back a poker room. The drinkers were ordinary men, almost all of them bearded, many of whom carried concealed weapons —revolvers for the most part. At the same time the bar was so nicely located and so pleasantly appointed that the professional men of the city not infrequently went there for a half-hour of relaxation, or for lunch, even.

I used to go into the place to see if anybody would like to buy a copy of the *Evening Herald,* five cents. Well, anyway, that was the excuse. I liked to go in there. I liked the long bar, the big framed mirrors behind it, the seminudes in great oil paintings, the flags of California and the United States, the smell, the spittoons, the hum of many men talking.

One afternoon a man nodded that he would like to have a paper, for which he gave me a silver dollar. I asked the bartender to please give me change, but the man said, "No, I want you to have that dollar." I was amazed and thanked the man, continued to ask others if they would like a copy of the paper—nobody did, and then I left the place. The following day I went back, but the man wasn't there and nobody in the place wanted a paper.

Every afternoon for weeks I went into the place at least once, sometimes twice, but nobody bought a paper. I really didn't mind, but I did remember the man who gave me a silver dollar for a paper, and I wondered if I would see him again. I didn't want him to give me another silver dollar. I just wanted to see him again. He was a plain man, a farmer, a trapper, or an ordinary workingman. He was not a town man, not a professional man.

I never saw him again, I can't even remember anything especially unique about him, except perhaps his heartiness, although I don't believe he was drunk. And nobody ever again gave me a dollar for a paper, or even half a dollar. One or two people gave me a quarter, though, and one evening in the rain E. Y. Foley bought

all of my papers, seven or eight, and gave me half a dollar for them, so I could go home and get out of the rain.

13. The Palace Theatre, Broadway, New York, 1928

THE EARLY YEARS WERE SO PACKED WITH EVERYTHING that one year seemed like a very long time, as of course it was. It is only when the years begin to repeat themselves that they seem to be gone almost instantly.

There is this that I want to say about my early years, not for myself alone, or for my writing alone, or for anybody in my family, or from a sense of responsibility about the matter, but simply because it is so—and something I don't want to forget. All of my time, the very earliest, the latest, the most recent, all of it, every instant of it has never been totally free of sorrow. The sorrow was second nature or innate or inevitable, it was there all the time: it gave a thoughtful brooding cast to the visage. There was almost never a complaint, because complaining was in bad taste, although that did not prevent me from having definite if private opinions about people who were plainly sons of bitches. Also there at all times, side by side with the sorrow, or possibly even a part of it, was humor—an awareness of air, light, sounds, smells, and unaccountable ideas.

And now and then a stunning surprise. A walking five-piece German band suddenly arrived at the front steps of the Orphanage and played a waltz—and I was hooked forever, not so much by music as by form. There it was, right in there, everything just so. I hadn't heard or noticed anything like it before.

41

And then all of a sudden it was August, 1928, and I was on a Greyhound bus going to New York for the first time in my life, perhaps the largest, grandest piece of travel in all of my experience. In Cleveland there was a wait of a couple of hours between buses, so I went to a theatre, and I couldn't believe what I saw—a white, almost naked woman danced in a strange way to strange music and took off spangled parts of a costume that concealed the final parts of her body: nipples, flat belly, and round bottom. The revelation was blinding and gave a boy a baseball bat in his pants, a dry mouth, and an insatiable lust for the voluptuous body. And that just wouldn't do, although there lingered in the troubled soul the feeling that nothing else would.

Soon after I reached New York, I found the Palace Theatre on Broadway, paid a quarter, went to the top balcony, to the last row, and sat down, as James Barton sang *Laugh, Clown, Laugh*. Well, this *was* my theatre, American vaudeville was my theatre.

I just sat back and let the happy variety happen. I just sat there and felt absolutely great, and home.

14. The Public Library, Fresno, 1921

GOING, LEAVING ONE PLACE TO GET TO ANOTHER, ALWAYS seemed vital and basic to me. For a new man, Fresno was no place to linger. Since I couldn't go in person, by train or car, I went in spirit, by book, and so the Public Library became a kind of depot for me. My time was not my own, I was not free to go there after school or any time I cared to. There were always other things to do that came first. These things had to do with earning money, so that the five of us in the family might be able to improve our lot, little by little: Takoohi—the widow since 1911 of Armenak Saroyan—and the four kids.

We all worked whenever there was work, or whenever we could invent it, as when I told J. D. Tomlinson I could sweep and mop the whole Telegraph Office and wash the window every morning before going to school —for about half of what he had been paying. Or when somebody else in the family pointed out to somebody else a sensible work, and was invited to do the work— for very low wages, of course. When such work was not available, there was work at home: the chickens had to have plenty of grass, and it was fetched from where it grew abundantly. The two barns had to be put in order, and Henry and I did that work. The thousands of old English walnuts from the majestic tree in the backyard had to be separated from their black dry casings, so

43

that breaking them might be an activity of reasonable tidiness. And so on.

But no matter how much work a man does, I soon learned, there is still plenty of time left over for other things—to sit at a table and eat, for instance. To sleep. And even in the very midst of work to loaf. So it was a matter of using time sensibly, and I got the knack of that quite early.

There were long hours between working hours which had to be used up. The empty lot next to the house at 2226 San Benito Avenue was the arena of all manner of games involving the boys of Armenian Town. This made it possible to get in a good ten or fifteen minutes before supper, for instance—which would not have been possible had we gone to the California Playground, six blocks away.

But soon enough the place of transport, of take-off, of travel, became the Public Library, where stuff from all over the country came every day and week and month: newspapers, magazines, and books. I sampled them all.

I browsed among the floor-to-ceiling rows of books for hours, reading around in perhaps forty or more books before the used-up air of the place, and the narrowness of the aisles between the rows, and the stuff in the books, drove me back out into the streets, which suddenly seemed alive with stuff better than stuff in books—the bread and onion and water of intelligence itself.

15. House in Millneck, Long Island, 1947

THE OWNER OF THE PLACE WAS A RETIRED ADMIRAL OR something of that kind. There was a dry pool and a snowbound tennis court, and dense woods, and hired help that he passed along to winter tenants—he took the place back in the season, as I believe it is called.

The arrangements of renting had been made by the little woman's little mother, who was good at that sort of thing—the rent was extremely high, the cost of the help was extremely high, the fuel required to keep the large house hot in all of its rooms was a full tank of oil about every ten days, the food bills were incredibly high, and it was the kind of place the little woman and her little mother had chosen because it was perfect for the giving of parties.

The Millneck part of the address was smart, and the place itself, always in meticulous order, was just right for anywhere from six to sixty people at a party. Everybody knew that after three years in the Army and two years back in society, so to put it, I was broke and in debt, but this reality was acknowledged only now and then when far gone in alcohol and pushing to another orgasm with the little woman she said, "What are we going to do?"

We?

Well, of course she and her little mother always believed—why, for that boy money is the easiest thing in the world to make, by the hundreds of thousands of dollars.

They were both not unlike literary agents, or more accurately Hollywood agents. They put packages together, even in idle social conversation. They were good at throwing around the titles of some of my novels and plays in relation to various motion picture companies, producers, directors, actors and actresses, but they spoke from ignorance. They had not read any of the plays or novels. They *could* read, but they read only the newspapers, and only the columns—to which the little woman's little mother leaked news that was useful to her.

Between the mother and the daughter, they knew everybody, or so they seemed to imply. And whenever there was a big party at the house in Millneck a fair assortment of these people put in an appearance—the most preposterous couples I had ever seen, but by that time I was always safely drunk, although able to give the impression that I was there, that I was giving the party, that the place was my house. Which was pure performance on my part. I had nothing to do with any of it. I just happened to be married to the little woman, and she just happened to be who she was, which she knew and I didn't, and her mother happened to be who she was, and there was this son of almost four, and this daughter of two, to complicate the situation, and to assure the little woman and her little mother ideal economic and legal advantage, no matter what happened, and of course they knew the worst was bound to

happen, and in fact sometimes seemed impatient to see it happen. The little woman's little mother was married to a man of some substance, about thirty years her senior, who was said to be insured for a million dollars.

I had six months of high society and then the lease
ran out.

16. The Typing Class
at Tech High, Fresno, 1921

IT WAS AN INSIDE ROOM SOMEWHERE IN AN OLD BUILDING, but not entirely inside. I have tried to sleep in rooms entirely inside, and it is the first thing one notices about them, and remembers forever. There was one window looking out to light, but to only a little light, because of a wall a few feet off from the window, and in any case the window was small.

In the room there were six rows of desks, each row with six desks, making a total of thirty-six desks, each with a big typewriter upon it, with the keys blacked out, so that the students would learn Touch Typing—in short, you were there to learn to type without needing to look for the keys, your fingers were to be trained so that you needn't bother about where to find the keys to spell any word, all you had to do was think of the word, and automatically your fingers would type it. In order to be permitted to take the typing course a student was required also to take the shorthand course—Gregg's. In other words, office workers were being taught the skills that would get them better wages and more important and interesting work.

Writers were not being prepared for their precarious careers. But I was in the class solely (if privately) in order to improve my chances of becoming a great writer.

I was never prepared to believe I would be anything other than that. Either I was a great writer or forget it. If I broke through, that was the deciding factor. And in order to expect to break through, I needed to be able to get my writing on paper in good easy-to-read form, and as quickly as possible. Well, certainly quicker than if I wrote the stuff in longhand and then looked around for somebody to type it for me, and for the money to pay for the typing. That procedure just wouldn't do for me.

And so in my 13th year, in the Spring of 1921, I went to a lot of trouble and ran into a lot of opposition in the matter of getting transferred from Longfellow Junior High to Tech High. The woman in charge of Transfers was required to ask why I wanted to transfer. I said I wanted to learn typing, which impelled her to ask *why* I wanted to learn typing.

I couldn't tell her the truth, so I said, "I'm going to need it in looking for work."

Whenever such people ask me questions, I tend to get hot and frequently begin to say insulting things about the public education system, the city, the state, and the nation. I can't help it, Governments are kept cluttered with unfinished business by the millions of clerks they must hire, and this is the only way for governments to stay in business, but whenever one or another of the clerks starts asking me questions about something that is my business alone, or begins to tell me what I can do and what I can't, I get hot. But the woman finally let me have the Transfer slip.

I went to the typing class every morning for almost two full months before typing became automatic.

If I thought a word, my fingers typed it. If I thought

a sentence, my fingers typed the sentence. If I had in mind a whole paragraph, my fingers kept right up with my thinking. That was one of the big achievements of my early life in Fresno. And I loved the break-through and the skill that came with it.

Nothing could stop me now.

17. The George V Hotel, Paris, 1959

I ARRIVED AT THE GEORGE SANK HOTEL, AS IT'S CALLED BY the rich Americans who insist on going there, late in March or early in April of the year 1959, after taking a train from Malibu to New York, and a ship from New York to Venice, from whence I went by train to Belgrade, where I paid $1,400 cash for an almost new Karmann-Ghia, which I drove to Zagreb, Rijeka, Trieste, Genoa, San Remo, Monaco, Nice, Cannes, and finally north to Paris, where I really didn't want to go.

I had been to the George Sank several times before. I knew it was expensive, but I didn't care about that, because I had lost all the money I had in the world in the casinos of the Riviera, and I had driven to Paris with the specific if unhappy intention of earning by very hard work the money I had lost, and also money with which to pay my back taxes, and so I didn't want to save eight or nine dollars a day by going to a cheap hotel somewhere.

I really hated being in Paris, and I wasn't very happy about not having bought a vineyard somewhere along the Riviera. I had been drinking and gambling steadily for a good three or four weeks, and so I went right on drinking. And gambling. And smoking two or three packs of cigarettes a day from the time I got up in the morning to the time I went to sleep, again in the morning.

Was I killing myself? No, but somebody was, or something was, and I wanted to work my way to a little peace. I bought National Lottery tickets, hoping to win the money I needed, but I didn't win.

I then telephoned the famous movie producer Darryl Zanuck and we met and talked and I drank heavier than ever.

I wrote a play for him, and we bargained, and he had his hatchet men phone or visit and talk and bargain, and in the end he paid $60,000 for the movie rights to the play.

I wrote the play in ten or eleven days at the George Sank Hotel—room 808, about $18 a day. I worked very hard, fighting out the form and style of the play, and then went out to drink and gamble.

One night in May I ran into a Hollywood agent named Charles Feldman in the lobby of the George Sank. I answered his question as to where I was going by saying, "To the Aviation Club."

"Are you *still* gambling?" he said.

And I just couldn't find the words with which to tell him everybody I knew was making big money without any more effort than a few phone calls and a few meetings, while I was still writing.

"Yes," I said. "It seems to help me stay at my work."

18. Typewriter Shop, 6th Avenue at 44th Street, New York, 1928

THE FIRST THING I NEEDED IN NEW YORK WAS A TYPE-writer, so I went looking around for a store that sold them. As luck would have it, I found a small place on 6th Avenue and the owner himself showed me what he had—new and secondhand. I decided to take a Corona, brand-new for $60. It was sturdy, it was light, and the type was large and clean. A good secondhand machine was about $30, but I had a good personal reason for buying the new machine: It was to be the machine on which I was to do the writing that would make my name. (In a matter of one evening, it sometimes seemed to me. For a long time I imagined that I would suddenly write something so right it would get me straight to the top, famous and rich.) The man was slim, pleasant, a New Yorker, a Jew, easygoing, friendly, and absolutely no high pressure about him at all.

"Have I got the best machine for the money?" I said. And he said, "The best, who knows the best, but it is a very good machine, and I think it will do the job." And then he said, "You're from someplace. Where?"

"Just got in from San Francisco, by bus."

"I thought so. How is life out there?"

"About the same as here, I guess—if you're there."

A few days later I dropped by again to buy another ribbon for the typewriter, as I had done a lot of new writing, none of it quite what it ought to be, and I had written letters to members of the immediate family, and to one or two friends—long letters, real letters, letters of great importance, as a matter of fact—but there it is, the friends read the letters and threw them away. The letters to members of the family were kept of course, because that is how it is with families.

Somehow the man in the typewriter shop got to talking about the local and national elections coming up, and he said, "There is a man to watch. Probably be the Governor of New York some day. Lehman." Well, of course I didn't care about that at all. I didn't care about any politician. I considered them all frauds, including the great ones: Washington, Lincoln, and Jackson. But of course a lot of people wouldn't even put Andrew Jackson with the other two, and in point of time he came before Lincoln. I put him there because at school there was a badly drawn picture of Jackson sharing acorns with a tired soldier under a tree—the soldier didn't know he was in the presence of General Andrew Jackson. I liked the sharing of the acorns and the keeping of the eminence to himself. Jackson was as big a fraud as any of the other politicians. You can't be with any government and not be thereby compromised forever. But I remembered the 6th Avenue man's prediction about an unknown man named Lehman. And when Lehman became Governor of New York I said to myself, "That guy on 6th Avenue in 1928, he was right. Lehman *did* become Governor of New York."

19. Danish Creamery,
Fresno Street, Fresno, 1922

THIS PLACE WAS COOL, THAT'S ALL. IT WAS COOL. IT WAS spotlessly clean. It was a place in which you had to feel good. The Danes had gone to Fresno about the same time as the Armenians, but instead of seizing upon the advantages of vineyards and orchards the Danes had gone right on in the dairy business.

The Danish Creamery products were the best—they had won ribbons and cups and medals and parchments at the biggest fairs and at the smallest. They knew their business and they liked it. And so across the street from the Hippodrome Theatre, where the program was a movie, a newsreel, a short comedy, and an hour of vaudeville—the best show in town, by far—the Danes opened a store where you could watch the girls shape and wrap butter in quarter-pound cubes, or in one-pound slabs. And where you could buy cream, milk, eggs, cottage cheese, and excellent-quality bread like rye and pumpernickel. But I went to the Danish Creamery on Fresno Street for something else they sold.

The creamery-faced girls with the creamery-bare arms stood behind the marble counter on which rested, always, four big glass pitchers of buttermilk. Real buttermilk, full of little specks and chunks of golden butter. On the counter were fresh, cool, clean glasses. Also large salt shakers, also of glass. Everything fresh and cool and clean, and not one fly, not even a baby fly, in the place. There was a sign, which was hardly required: "Fresh Buttermilk, All You Can Drink, 5¢." Well, of course in the summertime, in the months of May, June, July, August, September, and October—and for that matter in all of the months of the year—drinking buttermilk was a beautiful thing. It was just what the doctor ordered.

I rode up on my bike every afternoon when I was good and thirsty, went in, put my nickel on the marble bar, filled my glass, sprinkled salt on it, and drank it down. I waited half a moment, not more than three or four seconds, and did it again, and further up along the counter a Judge of the Superior Court was doing the same thing, why shouldn't I, a messenger?

I never drank less than three glasses, and frequently as many as six or even seven.

The slim belly tightened and tried to bulge out somewhere, and I felt renewed, went out, got on my bike, and went back to work.

I remember this place continuously. I really lived in there. Hot, hot, hot everywhere in the world. The body moving at the business of pushing a bike all over the town, the juices going dry, the sweat pouring out of the skin—six glasses of buttermilk, cool, cool, and a man of thirteen or fourteen was ready to hit the road again, cheering Denmark.

20. 3rd Avenue Penthouse, New York, 1963

IT WAS AT THE TOP OF A NEW RICKETY BULLSHIT BUILDING on 3rd Avenue, and I saw the small apartment long before the building was finished. With me was one of my many cousins, one of the busy rich ones. Having run into him on 5th Avenue I had brought him along to look at the place.

"Take it," he said. "Six hundred a month for three years is nothing. Nobody can get a room at a decent hotel for six hundred a month any more, so what can you lose? When you're not in New York, let friends or family use it, or sublet it, or let it stay empty."

The reasoning seemed sound, so after I had gone up and looked at the place another couple of times over a period of a month I signed the lease and paid the usual three or four months in advance—occupancy guaranteed by February 1st of the following year, 1963.

A New York penthouse on 3rd Avenue, no less—overlooking the East River, the Queensboro Bridge, Astoria across the river in Long Island, and other junky places. There was a good six months before occupancy, so I went about my business, traveling to California, and up and down the Coast, and then late in January I checked into a hotel in New York, and went to see the penthouse—my own penthouse. Wow, I'd have beautiful girls coming up there to sleep with me. But of course I'd lock the terrace doors before they went to bed, so they wouldn't be able to rush out there impetuously when I told them no, I wasn't going to marry them, and jump to 3rd Avenue, twenty-two floors below.

Well, even in mid-February the whole building was still under construction, so to put it.

The owner (there were actually three of them, each very rich) had very new, very narrow, very highly polished black shoes on his feet.

He was always about somewhere, egging the Superintendent on, a little added chore here, another there, and surely the building would open on schedule, in eight days.

But this business of the narrow shoes, highly polished, is worth a moment longer: such shoes are worn almost as a religious rite by an order of man of the world who may best be described as a self-deceived success.

I got into the joint a month late, and was astonished to find that it had a humming noise coming from the ceiling and the walls, and that the whole apartment vibrated all the time.

The hum and the vibration were the consequence of having directly overhead large and heavy machinery that worked night and day to heat the whole building, or to send cool air into every apartment during the hot weather.

I tried to work in the place, but the noise and vibration made writing impossible. When I left, at a great loss of time and money, the man in the highly polished shoes sued me.

It cost me new money to fight him off, but he quit

like a dog and went back to his narrow shoes, his narrow success, and his narrow wealth.

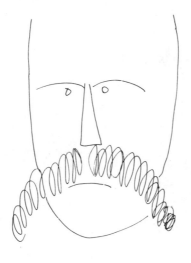

21. The Bahai Temple, Haifa, 1961

AT A PARTY IN LONDON IN 1944 MR. ERNEST HEMINGWAY ridiculed the man whose guest he was, saying, "He pretends that that's his girl, so nobody will know he's a fairy." And Mr. Arthur Koestler, virtually resting his head on Mr. Hemingway's shoulder and looking up into his eyes with unfeigned adoration, did not speak up for his friend, with whom at a Greek Restaurant a month earlier he had dominated, bullied, and bored a group of six or seven writers, mostly American, vollying back and forth between them sarcastic words about the others.

"The writer must know everything," the little man had said, by which he meant that *he* did, he knew everything, and that the others were stupid bums.

And the host, with his thick head and weary confusion, had added, "It is not enough merely to write."

So a month later here was the big bearded American calling him a fag, and here was the belittled man's best buddy (in snobbism) adoring the big boy. As for myself, I was amazed. What was the matter with these men, these writers, heterosexual, homosexual, bisexual, nonsexual, or whatever the hell they might be? Why were they such horse's asses?

Well, the scene changed, the world changed, everybody went home, I went home, it wasn't home, I didn't know whether I was going or coming, I couldn't write,

I couldn't think, the telephone was busy all day and all night, somebody was calling the little woman, or she was calling somebody, every half-hour.

And then in a London Sunday paper one day I read a big essay by Arthur Koestler about his recent visit to the newly formed nation called Israel. And I remembered him, both at the Greek Restaurant in London and at the party given by his friend, a far better writer than himself.

Apparently unintentionally, he made Israel seem to be the scene of the hope of the world.

And so one year, by that time divorced, broke, up the creek, damaged beyond repair by the war, the Army, an unfortunate marriage, desperation, impulsiveness, gambling, drinking, I decided to visit Israel, too. A ship stopped at Haifa, and I was told the best hotel in town was the Dan, up the hill. After I was settled, I walked down the hill and came to a place with fine gardens inside a high metal picket fence, and as the gate was open I went in.

It was the Bahai Temple. It was the Main Office of International Bahai, a very nice religion without much of an image, with no hero, or at any rate no hysterical hero, no big show-biz trial, no fancy parables, no crucifixion, just a man who sincerely believed there *was* a nice way for *everybody* to live.

I met a number of the people who either ran the office or helped run it, and a number of visitors, or pilgrims. It was all nice, if lonely. But the grounds were beautiful and the building was beautiful, and the people were gentle losers.

I've always remembered that place. It was put there long ago, when the area was not called Israel.

I even went up to Acre, to the shrine of the founder

of the cult. The caretakers were a retired professor from Berkeley and his wife. There were roses in the garden, and rather lovely butterflies, as well as several long lizards. It was all hopeless and sad, while Israel was all business, but probably not quite the hope of the world.

22. The Lost Bordello, near the Opera, Paris, 1935

I was running up the Rue de la Paix, from sheer joy in being in Paris at last, in April of 1935, or I was running down Rue September 4, or I was running along Fauberge Montmartre, going in and out of places—the Hotel Scribe for instance, the Grand across the street from the Scribe, the inside area of the Café de la Paix, stores, travel agencies.

I was there, I myself, in person, not a dream, not a movie, and the world was a pretty girl I meant to get. I was sure Paris was the place to have her.

A girl fell in beside me, and I was amazed that she knew about my plan. She was very plain, a little sorrowful as a matter of fact, and clearly out of her element. Still, I liked her for directness and honesty. I suggested another time perhaps, but might it be possible that she could direct me to the best bordello in Paris, for I was a stranger in town, and I had money. I gave her a piece of paper money I imagined was worth a dollar or two. She was not offended, and walked with me seven or eight blocks to a rather handsome building. She smiled, and thanked me. I thanked her, and I went to the door and pressed a button.

The door was opened by a lacy lady of forty or fifty years, large of bosom and face and mouth and eye, and I knew this was the place.

She took me to a room about the size of a circus ring in which white horses trot around while men and women leap upon their backs and balance themselves gracefully. The entire room was finished in sparkling mirror, including the floor and ceiling.

Suddenly the most incredible event in the history of happy fulfillment of erotic fantasy took place: a whole school of girls, stark naked except for jewelry and shoes, came into the room, smiling, and stood in a circle around me. All of a sudden I had everything, as well as truth.

There were at least two dozen girls: blondes, redheads, brunettes, black-haired girls, white-skinned, rose-skinned, black, tan, yellow, and girls with great bodies and small breasts and others with small bodies and great breasts.

It was heaven. But it was hell trying to choose only one out of the dazzling lot. At last I chose a big girl, perhaps from Germany, but an instant before this choice became absolute and final I swung my arm away from the big girl to a small girl with a face that was made entirely out of love of amusement, perhaps from France.

We retired to a room with a bed, surrounded by mirrors. It was impossible not to watch, at least part of the time.

It was the best bordello I ever visited.

And the Madam and the girls were the best, because they were the happiest.

At the Madam's desk to pay the modest honorarium, it turned out that instead of having five dollars I had four. The Madam laughed and took three, leaving me one and vive la France.

23. Postal Telegraph Branch Office, 405 Brannan Street, San Francisco, 1927

George Horan at the Main Office asked me to drop by during my lunch hour, so I walked from the 651 Market Street Office to the Main Office on Battery. I was nineteen years old and I had several times asked George Horan to give me a job with more money.

George had a way of speaking softly and as if this were between the two of us, highly confidential, and a plot to frustrate the big shots in high places.

"I've got this Office over on Brannan," he said, "a block from the Southern Pacific. The manager's old and lazy and wants to go back to a night job as a telegrapher. Do you think you could take his place?"

I said I knew I could.

"Well," George went on, "there's a little catch. It's the same pay, twenty dollars a week, but if you can increase the business, you'll get a raise."

I opened the office the following morning at eight and closed it that evening at six. I took no lunch hour. I called on a dozen companies in which a Postal Telegraph call box had been installed, and I tested the call boxes to see that they were all in working order, phoning May McGarry at the Desk to let her know I would use a call box three times and for her to stay on the line and tell me where the call was coming from. She

65

did so. All the call boxes were working excellently, but one was completely out. This was reported to the proper department and a lineman went out to that company the next day and put the call box in working order.

It was a small telegraph office with a large district. To get out to John Deere Tractor I asked Sullivan, the motorcycle messenger, to give me a ride. I sat behind him. He took off like a shot, I sat in the street, and he circled around and came back laughing, while May McGarry came running to see if I was all right. I was, but not anywhere near as amused as Sullivan, one of those overgrown boys who love bikes and are killed in an accident before they reach the age of twenty-two.

In a week I checked all of the call boxes that hadn't been used in a week or so, which was about half of the three hundred that had been installed. I then began to call on the companies that were known to send a great many telegrams, and sure enough those which hadn't been sending any by Postal Telegraph began to do so, and those that had been sending only a few by Postal began to send more. Why? For the simple reason that somebody had gone and talked to them about the matter.

Business increased so much it was necessary to hire more messengers, and finally I put in a crew of eight Filipino messengers, because the other boys were too lazy for a big district like that. And the Filipinos were glad to have the work and to be all in the same office. May McGarry liked them, too, because they were so thoughtful and courteous. After only a month the business had been doubled. After two months it had been tripled. Still, George Horan said he hadn't been able to get an O.K. for a raise. Finally, I quit. The Money is stingy, but it really isn't anywhere near as clever as it thinks it is. Had The Money not revealed itself as a stupid thief, I might have lingered a year or two longer in the Business World.

24. 2226 San Benito Avenue, Fresno, 1921

IT WAS MY UNIVERSITY, IT WAS THE WORLD, IT WAS ART, IT was everything, a ramshackle frame house owned by a dour man named Barr who came on a bicycle once a year to repair little things and to see if the walls needed repapering. The rent was ten dollars a month—ten dollars for thirty or more days, for five people. The two barns, the old English walnut tree in the backyard, the sycamore on the alley side of the house, and the lilac bush out there shading the parlor window, loaded every spring with great clusters of purple-blue flowers, scenting the whole house with the smell of joy and expectation. And along the whole of the front porch the old honeysuckle, which had become a mighty clinging tree, loaded with blossoms to which came butterflies, moths, and best of all hummingbirds. Ten dollars a month for all that, but it was still no bargain, for the roof leaked in a dozen places if there was a heavy rainfall—if light, it leaked in only one or two, and pots and pans had to be put around under the drippings.

Well, there is this matter of houses, of housing, of where kids spend their early times, and it is a matter of importance. I have heard members of my own family say that where they lived, the house in which they grew up, embarrassed and shamed them deeply, so that their very natures were affected. But I do not remember ever having felt that way about any house in which I spent time, and, as I told one of my cousins when he brought the matter up, "How could I dislike my own house? I lived there. That made it as good a house as any anywhere."

Of course there was never a day during which the family did not believe that we would soon be moving out of that house to a better one, which we would not rent, which we would buy, and own—our own house. Still, the years at 2226 San Benito Avenue were some of the greatest of my life, for I grew from childhood to boyhood and to the beginnings of early manhood there, or at any rate the arrival of an awareness of sex in my life —a tiger to keep in the custody of the heart.

I was almost eight when I began to live in the wonderful house, and almost thirteen when we began to buy our own house at 3204 El Monte Way, about two miles east.

I made many discoveries and decisions in the rented house. The best of the lot, I suppose, was that I had a choice: I could make of my life and of myself anything that any man had ever made of himself. Therefore, it was a matter of making a choice as soon as possible and then going after it with all my muscle and mind. I chose writing. But did I? Might it not be just as accurate to say that I discovered that I was a writer and that therefore it would be foolish to choose another character, identity, labor, or life for myself?

It was a happy house, but let us never for a minute forget the complexity of truth, for it was a house in which dwelt also rage, sorrow, hatred, and madness itself.

25. 74 Rue Taitbout, Paris, 1969

YESTERDAY, FRIDAY, AUGUST 8TH, I DECIDED THAT AFTER having had a mustache for almost a full year, growing freely, never trimmed, and after having not had a haircut in three full months, I would take the barber shears I keep on my desk and reduce the mustache to a brush, and cut the hair of the head.

Does this seem impossible? It is no such thing. Does it seem foolish, in the sense that one is bound to make such a shambles of one's head that a barber will be required to straighten the matter out, after all, and that the barber will be impelled to ask, "What happened?"

Again no such thing. With only the shears and a small comb, I trimmed an enormous mustache to a very sensible, full, neat mustache, and I removed an enormous amount of black hair mixed with gray at the temples and in the sideburns from the head. I then shaved and used the safety razor to tidy up the back of the head at the neck. And then I got into a tub to have a shampoo and a shower.

The result was amazing. I was suddenly not so much somebody else as myself long ago, as in fact I had *seen* my face and head long ago, when I was thirty, for instance. Something had been lost in the all-around shearing, but I could well afford the loss, it was midsummer and very hot, and in a matter of three weeks I would have finished the 61st year of my time, so I rather enjoyed the giving of a general lightness to the face and head, and therefore also to the body and spirit.

And suddenly there he was, the writer, far from Bitlis where his people had lived until the turn of the century, and all of the men had worn moustaches precisely like the one he had just trimmed. And there he was far from Fresno where 61 years ago he had arrived in total forgetfulness, and had immediately begun to fight his way to the World and the Word. There he was, himself again, as he had been thirty years ago, the well-known total stranger.

Yesterday was a good day in Paris and the World, and very hot, with a wild glare. I moseyed along through two one-hour walks, drank gallons of cold water, and really didn't mind anything at all.

26. The Belasco Theatre, 44th Street, New York, 1941

LEE SHUBERT WAS A THIN LITTLE MAN WITH A PARCH-ment face and a very soft voice. I learned later that he was the sharpest Money Boy around, sharper even than Billy Rose and Billy's bitter enemy Mike Todd. I also learned that Mr. Shubert had enjoyed the favors, as I believe it is put, of a wide variety of young women eager to go on the stage, who were in fact frequently *permitted* to go on, in parade jobs, beautifully costumed, with feathers and spangles and tights, and later sent along to join Mr. Shubert somewhere for a cup of cocoa.

The Belasco Theatre was one of two dozen theatres he and his brother J. J. Shubert and perhaps another brother and perhaps an uncle or a mother or a nephew or somebody else partly owned. The theatre bore the name of the Deacon from San Francisco, Mr. David Belasco, a flamboyant man of the theatre, sometime playwright, and God of Trash—that is to say, a hero of the theatre and its crowd, always an odd lot.

It was a huge place, with perhaps 1,200 seats, and at the top of the second balcony I was shown around the old man's Private Nest—with its Peephole directly down to the stage, so he could keep his eye on how the hired help was performing another of his big hits: some of the most inept plays ever written, but in their day highly satisfying to the ticket-buyers.

72

It was a big, spacious nest and I tried to imagine myself up there with a gorgeous woman wanting to go on
the stage. It was easy to do, but the place was dusty,
haunted by a fraud who never suspected as much, and by
his banal ideas and his gorgeous women and girls. The
first thing a man ought to have in the theatre is an
insatiable capacity for enjoying the favors of desperate
women. Otherwise it were better to go into the Insur-
ance Game, as I once heard it referred to.

Mr. Shubert's feet were narrow and in very tight,
highly polished, expensive shoes. I had to notice this,
because I was eager to understand his dance, so to put
it, his style of movement, his way of walking, which was
slow and quite dainty. I was thirty-three years old in
1941 when a deal was made with Mr. Shubert involving
my usage of the long-empty and dusty Belasco Theatre
as the arena in which I would present a variety of my
plays.

Very quietly and in a very friendly manner Mr.
Shubert said, "I want you to know how pleased I am
that the Saroyan Theatre is to originate at the Belasco.
Any way that I can help, I am at your service. Go in
there with a free heart. Don't worry about business
matters."

But that wasn't what he meant at all, for when the
terms of the written agreement were technically faulted
because the box office intake fell below a certain number of dollars per week, again he came dancing slowly
to the theatre to tell me softly that he would be very
happy if I would vacate the theatre by the end of the
week, in accordance et cetera et cetera. He was quite a
dainty man.

73

27. The Empty Lot at
San Benito & M Street, Fresno,
1918

WELL, THE MOST IMPORTANT THING TO REMEMBER ABOUT the big empty lot which my brother Henry and I made into a playfield for the whole neighborhood was its ample size, and its varied vegetation, which consisted of plants of an extraordinarily hardy order—with thorns, thistles, and acrid scents. Desert plants several of them, and these plants still flourish in the outlying areas of Fresno. Whenever I come upon them, I stop and look at them and breathe in the scent that comes from them. One of the plants has a kind of resinous leaf, which always seems laden over with dust, which of course is not dust but its own composition. The scent is hard to describe—gaseous perhaps, oily, strong.

Every year Henry and I took shovels to the fresh growth of plants in the empty lot and brought them all down, smelling them as we did our work. The smell was hardly rosy. In fact to a young nose all of the San Benito lot plants had smells which might be considered bad. But the fact remains that fifty years later I find the smells appealing.

Why? How can that be?

Quite simple. I had known the smells long ago, they were part of my living experience, they brought back something. I cherished the plants and the smells both.

That's how it is with us. Even our worst enemies in time become precious.

The purpose of the lot was to give Henry and me access to quick athletic diversion, and no sooner were we out there playing tin-can hockey or pee-wee or throwing a ball back and forth than other boys of the neighborhood began to arrive, some of them bringing other athletic goods, such as a football or a basketball. From just across the San Benito alley, out of a house almost precisely like our own house, came Ralph and Yep Moradian. Ralph was Henry's age and Yep was mine, 11 and 8 when we first moved to the house. From across the street came Levon Kemalyan, also 11, and from the northeast corner house at M and San Benito came Elish and Vahan Shekoyan, also 11 and 8, and from N and San Benito came Fat Khashkhash. From M Street near the railroad freight crossing, hardly ever used by trains, came Vahan and Eddie Bazoyan. From M and Santa Clara came Joe and Al Kalakian, Johnny and Joe Elia, and Lionel Simonian. From L Street came Joe Sargis, an Assyrian, and from just across from the Emerson School playground came Eddie Emerian, and Charley Barsom.

On M Street, at the top end of the empty lot, was the home of John Kovacevich and his son Johnny, from Slovenia. There were many others who now and then dropped by to take part in a game, but these others were from other neighborhoods: Mark and Al Nidevar, Willie Ryan, and many boys who were so poor at games that one didn't even bother to learn their names. The neighborhood hero was Jim Lundy, about 18, who was an all-around athlete, very strong and very friendly.

Every Spring in the empty lot, there they were again, the powerful desert plants shooting up into handsome forms with strong branches .and leaves and blossoms, making a clean smell that I never suspected might some-day seem to be the best smell I would ever breathe into my lungs.

One of these plants is appropriately called the Creosote Bush.

28. Guggenheim's Water Tank, Fresno, 1921

THE TANK WAS AT THE TOP OF A TIMBER DERRICK AMONG the Santa Fe Railroad tracks, at the end of San Benito Avenue. The timber was old and rickety. The ladder rungs had been nailed to the frame long ago. The nails had rusted, and some were loose. In one place, midway, a rung was missing. The climber going up had to put some muscle into it, and coming down he had to see that he didn't slip. The water tank had had a sign saying that it was against the law to climb the tower, but somebody had sensibly removed the sign.

One summer I climbed the tower a couple of times a week, once to drop a cat, which landed on its feet, bounced, and ran away at full speed. I was never mean to animals, and on this occasion I was more stupid than mean. I really believed the cat would not be injured in the fall. Perhaps it wasn't. All the same I have always felt a little guilty about having dropped the cat. And ashamed.

The railroad tracks and the eucalyptus trees among the tracks, in the Jungle, where the hoboes rested and cooked their stew and smoked cigarettes and talked, black and white alike, but never immigrants, never people who came to America to make good, the railroad tracks had cat packs, old toms, females, and half-grown young cats, all lean, all tough, all dirty. The cat I had taken up with me and had dropped from the top of the tower was one of these—a cat which had been trusting, unlike most of the others in the pack, which were suspicious of human beings, and afraid of them. This cat considered me a friend, and there it was—I betrayed the cat. I dropped it to hard ground from a height of at least a hundred feet.

And I had to be clever to do it, for the cat clung to my arm, and spoke, not piteously but rather bravely, as if to say, "You're not going to do something stupid, are you?"

I had to turn quickly and let the cat go. Even while it was tumbling head over heels and the boys who were with me, watching, cheered and laughed, I thought, "Please spare the poor animal, and I will never do such a stupid thing again."

I was thrilled when the cat struck the hard ground *lightly,* feet first, and bounced so swiftly that it was almost as if it had not in fact had a real impact with the ground, and then raced away. The escape and survival of the cat thrilled me deeply, because it made my mischief something less than a criminal act upon life.

The climbing to the top of the tower, then walking around the tank and looking around at the whole small town in all directions, and the climbing down, required concentration and care. It was all very definitely very dangerous. Why did I do it, then?

Because I believed in my ability to do it. After having done it, I actually was able to feel I had accomplished something of some importance to me.

29. The Great Northern Hotel, 118 West 57th Street, New York, 1935

I ARRIVED IN NEW YORK FOR THE FIRST TIME IN AUGUST OF 1928, a few days before my 20th birthday, and I walked in many parts of Manhattan, and in a number in Brooklyn. I took the subway to Coney Island, and to many other places, and went up the subway stairs to a new world, to look around.

During my walks up or down 57th Street, I passed the narrow entrance to The Great Northern Hotel many times and several times noticed the name and liked it, but I did not take a room there until 1935, after my first book had been published, and I was famous, or people believed I was, or I was able to imagine that I was, if not famous, then at least well-known. I went to The Great Northern Hotel after I had tried staying at The New Yorker Hotel on 34th and 8th Avenue where the rooms are very small.

I was delighted to be at The Great Northern, for the rooms were large, the bath was large, the ceilings were high, and (this may be difficult to believe) the rent was $12 a week. From a room on the fifth floor, number 512 I believe, an inside room with a poor view, I did the planning for my first trip to Europe, and I did some writing.

For instance, I read in *The New York Times* that I had recently arrived in New York, and that I was writing a play which I expected to finish before sailing to Europe. How or where the *Times* had gotten this misinformation I can't imagine, but I decided, "Well, if *The New York Times* says I'm writing a play, why not? Why make a liar out of *The New York Times*? Write a play."

In 1928 I made many notes about the writing of what I believed was to be my first novel, and perhaps one of the best things I would ever write, to be called, simply, *The Subway*. Meaning of course the New York subway, but also meaning the concealed way, the inside way, the hidden truth, the hidden life, the hidden meaning of people, of passengers, not of the subway alone, but of time, riding to the end of the line. But alas, this great book was never written.

Why?

I don't know. How could I know? It just wasn't. And I have always regretted that it wasn't.

So now, in 1935, seven years later, seven incredibly difficult, swift, dangerous, great, sorrowful, and laughing years later, back in New York, I remembered the book I failed to write, and I decided to see if I could do something or other with the subway in the form of a play, and so in a matter of three days I wrote *Subway Circus*. It has been published, it has been produced by amateurs, but I have never seen a production. And so the report on the theatre page of *The New York Times* turned out not to be, not to have been, inaccurate, after all.

I loved being at The Great Northern Hotel, and I

went back to the hotel again and again when I was in
New York—until at last it just wouldn't do any more:
the hotel had changed, I had grown more worldly, I
had become wealthy, and the world itself had changed,
so I moved on and up, as the saying is.

30. Governors Island, New York Harbor, 1943

IT IS A BIG JOKE TO MANY PEOPLE WHEN SOMEBODY TALKS with annoyance about the dirty tricks of the Army, because the feeling is, "Big deal, thousands have been killed, so tell us all about your hard times with the Army."

The fact is that one is bored by the Army even while one is putting up with its treachery. The worst kind of officer was the Medical. He was a clever, calculating son of a bitch. Play ball and you would be O.K. He would write an exemption that would prevent anybody from giving you dirty or hard work. Play better ball and he'd write you a medical discharge—a little gift of some sort, say one thousand dollars under the table, to a confederate, no strings attached, or if the drafted man happened to be loaded, a sum two or three times as large.

I was drafted with a bad upper-leg or low-back condition, which when it was acute was the most painful thing in my limited experience of pain—it was as violent and intense as the pain of a bad tooth, but this pain was in an area a hundred times larger. General tiredness, anxiety, frustration, anger, and all of the other negative states of the human mind and spirit tended to bring on an acute phase of the condition, whereupon I would be in serious trouble. I couldn't stand, let alone march, or work, or run.

Like a great many drafted men who were in the Army

in the New York area, I was permitted to live off the Post in my own apartment, which happened to be at 2 Sutton Place South, not far from the Queensboro Bridge, which I crossed early every morning in a taxi—whereupon my little bride, pregnant, went back to sleep until noon.

I stood in the six o'clock Roll Call Formation, answered to my name, and had half an hour to go get breakfast. I did not eat in the Army mess, the smell made me want to vomit, it did not smell like the world, it smelled like a loathsome sore on a great sick body. I hurried two blocks to a little all-night place run by a Jewish family and had a bagel and coffee while I looked through the *Times*. Then I went to the day's labor.

One morning at five I couldn't get out of bed: the slipped disk of the lower spine was out of place, and I was in terrible trouble. I telephoned the Sergeant at the Astoria Army Post, and after a little chat he said, "Well, come in when you can." Around noon I was able to move a little, and by two I went out to the Post, and checked in. The Sergeant, who confessed that before he got into the Army he sold shoes in a department store, wanted to know if I appreciated what he had done. I said I did, but he didn't mean that kind of appreciation. A month later I couldn't get out of bed again, so again I phoned, and I believed the situation was the same as last time, but around eleven two Military Police, two Medical Corps Sergeants, and two privates all came up to the penthouse at 2 Sutton Place South.

They were only following orders. I was to be taken to Governors Island. This was plainly a dirty trick. It was retaliation, because I had not rewarded anybody for letting me get to the Post half a day late. I was invited to lie upon the stretcher, but I forced myself to walk, and I was deposited in the hospital on Governors Island. A ratty place, with a great round stockade, or Army jail. And for all practical purposes I was in jail— apparently for desertion. I spent a week there, and was then transferred to another, bigger, Army hospital on Staten Island, and after a month of more chickenshit I was sent back to the same place in the Army. I wasn't playing the game. So I was being given the business.

31. The Bijou Theatre, J Street, Fresno, 1918

THE BIJOU WAS NOT PRONOUNCED AS A FRENCHMAN would say the word for a small jewel, it was pronounced Byjoe, and if anybody pronounced it any other way, nobody would know what he was referring to. It was in the very heart of Fresno, on J Street, above Mariposa, in the middle of the block, on the west side of the street. It was a silent movie threatre in the shape of a store, and not a very big store at that, but when you paid a dime for a ticket and went in, there was an aisle down the center of the auditorium, if that's what it might be called. There were four seats on either side of the aisle, and about thirty rows, down to where the piano was played by a man who knew his business. He knew when to play *Wedding of the Winds,* or something from *La Forza del Destino,* or *Roses of Picardy.* If jam-packed, the theatre could contain about 240 souls, and they were invariably kids—boys, that is, although now and then a tough, brave group of girls might try being in the theatre, and they might succeed for half an hour or so, whereupon they would sneak out. It was no place for girls.

The boys ate sunflower seeds continuously, said amusing and clean dirty things to one another in Armenian, Italian, Mexican, and Russian, which was actually German: the boys were *simply* called Rooshians. Now and then a whole Indian family with small kids would take two rows on one side of the aisle, and they would not mind the loud talk, the shouts, the jeers, the whistles, the various noises boys made when on the screen kissing took place, for instance, or a dirty rat tried to drive a nice old mother to the poorhouse, ar a big powerful man began to lay into a sensitive kindly man, who in the end kicked the shit out of the bully.

But essentially the Bijou was a boy's movie house and the management knew it, and booked pictures designed to please boys, cowboy stories, Tarzan stories, action stories, and comedies. And a big newsreel. There was a toilet up front beyond the piano. If you stayed to see the whole show, you were there for at least four hours, starting at nine Saturday morning, ten weekday mornings, and stopping around midnight. In short, the program was shown three times, but frequently something in one of the movies was so good that some of the groups would see the whole show twice, and this meant that everybody got hungry. The theatre understood boys and permitted them to leave the theatre for a few minutes to buy something to eat, generally a candy bar to supplement the enormous supply of sunflower seeds every boy had in his pockets. A whole big bag cost a dime, and four boys working steadily for four hours couldn't possibly run through all of them—about two pounds of them. Cracking the seed in the front teeth, spitting out the shell, and chewing the kernel were a perfect activity for being at the movies.

I spent many happy hours at the Bijou, but not nearly as many as most of the kids from the various slums of Fresno, for I always had work to do, chores to attend to, and I didn't often have four hours free in one chunk. I ducked in for an hour or two now and then, though, between chores. A lot of kids just couldn't afford the dime to get in, and they sneaked in. I did, too. Many times, both from the front and from the back of the theatre, from the alley. I don't know who the management happened to be, and while it pretended to frown on sneaking in, I don't think it ever really cared too much about stopping it. The fact is, the Bijou is the only theatre I have ever experienced that seemed to belong to the audience. I have dreamed about it as the arena of freedom itself.

32. The Berengaria, New York to Southampton, 1935

IT WAS MY FIRST OCEAN CROSSING, IN LATE MARCH OR early April, 1935. I was on my way to Europe. The ship was one of the biggest in the world, one of the biggest ever built, about 70,000 tons, the Cunard Line's *Berengaria*. I was traveling third class, and proud of it—not proud of being poor, I was proud of being rich, rich enough to get on such a boat at all, and proud to be on my way to Europe.

The whole thing was such an excitement that it was impossible for me even to think of trying to go to sleep. Around three in the morning everybody had disappeared and I was alone in a great room, and very hungry. A little worker of some kind, a cockney who must have been fifty-seven to my twenty-seven, came along, and I said, "I'm kind of hungry. Where can I buy something to eat?"

He said, "Stay here. I'll bring you a sandwich."

He was gone about fifteen minutes and came back with a silver tray loaded with ham and cheese sandwiches. I gave him a tip, and fell to. After a moment I began to be thirsty and looked around for something to drink, and then he came back with another tray, saying, "You couldn't eat sandwiches and not drink, so here's milk, bottle water, and ginger ale. Take your choice."

"I'll drink them all," I said.

"That's what they're for," he said, and went away.

I just sat and ate and drank and thought, and I think that that half-hour was one of the happiest, somberest, most melancholy, most loving of my life—I loved everybody and everything, and felt sorry for the lot.

33. Southern Pacific Train, Oakland to Fresno, 1915

ON A DAY OF SUMMERTIME BRIGHTNESS, I COULDN'T QUITE remember the stages by means of which I had finally arrived at the Oakland Depot to get on a train and go home—home: I had no memory of a real home so far: I had memories only of the place we were all four of us now leaving forever.

The occasion wasn't joyous, by any means. The party in charge, Cosette, 16 years old, had had a dispute with the Orphanage executive department, and she was still outraged by their dishonesty, ingratitude, and stupidity. They in turn had spoken harshly of herself, and the rest of us, and of all our relatives in the world. I didn't know any of that. I only knew I was going home, we were all going home, and home was two hundred miles south, a place called Fresno.

When I saw the locomotive come up, I was awed by the size and power, noise, blackness, and mystery of it.

We hoisted two suitcases and a couple of bundles onto the platform, and then made a double place for ourselves in the chair car and sat down. When the train began to go, I turned around—was it to see if they were following us, and would try to make us go back? Or was it simply to say, "Good-by and good riddance," or was it perhaps to say, "What years, what years passed there."

The train began to go and an optical game began: I watched stationary things reach my vision and then become cut off suddenly—trees, telephone poles, lamp-posts, automobiles, people on foot, buildings, houses, churches, and then open country with meadows all golden with mustard blossoms, and other meadows with splashes of wild flowers, and great round cement tanks that read, "Standard Oil Co." After a long time I asked Henry, "What does 'Co.' mean?" He told me Company, but I preferred "Co." with its mystery.

At Tracy somebody said, "We're halfway there."

I went to sleep, perhaps the happiest I have ever been, but also the most deeply aware of the sorrow at the center of everybody and everything.

I woke up soon and was offered an orange, which I peeled and ate. This seems to be something that must. happen during train travel.

What was my life? What was my life to be *now*? Well, I would have to wait and see.

At the Southern Pacific Depot in Fresno there was a man waiting to take us in his car to his house on a vineyard in Malaga, where Takoohi Saroyan was spending a few days, and where we would spend a few, too: he was Dikran Bagdasarian, husband of my mother's young sister Verkine. I have always deeply cherished this man, all of his 88 years. He was there.

"Hello, boys and girls," he said. "Come with me."

We went with him, and gladly.

34. Blood of the Lamb
Gospel Church, Turk Street
off Fillmore, San Francisco, 1929

IN 1929, AFTER MY RETURN FROM FAILURE IN NEW YORK, I used to seek free diversion wherever I might be able to find it, for the simple reason that I did not have the price of any other kind, and so I learned to find restoration of the soul in walking, looking at people and houses and animals and trees, or in visiting the places to which admission was both free and eagerly sought: the Public Library, the museums, the art galleries, the department stores, and the churches.

The Blood of the Lamb Gospel Church was actually an empty store on Turk Street. The plate-glass windows were whitened with Bon Ami, so that the services might be conducted in private. From the third-floor flat at 2378 Sutter Street the little store-church was a leisurely evening's walk of under fifteen minutes. After supper I frequently set out for a walk of restoration, thought, and peace, having in mind that I might just go into the little church and take a chair in the last row, and look and listen for a while. It was a church founded by several black people, and one frequently heard grateful references to Brother Hutchins, Elder Montgomery, Gospel Singer Sister Ellison, and Sexton Graves. There was no preacher, as such, or rather there was no official or ordained minister. But everybody seemed to be equal to giving either a testimonial about his life and transformation, a reading with asides from the Good Book, a loud prayer, a very lively dance, or a recitation in Tongues.

It was this last, which I heard and witnessed by good luck on my very first visit in January of 1929, that sent me back, in the hope that I might see and hear another version of it. The man who had been Talking in Tongues before my arrival was standing, his fists clenched, his eyes shut, sweat rollowing down his tan face. It took me two or three minutes to understand that he was not preaching, not praying, and not testifying—and furthermore that he was not speaking English, Spanish (which I imagined he *was* speaking, from the sound and rhythm and usage of the words): French, Italian, German, or any other language spoken by mortals. He was speaking in the language of the angels. He was possessed. I found that I did not consider that he was sick or mad. On the contrary, although he looked pretty wrought up, I felt that he was a kind of genius, a little freakish but no less authentic on that account. He talked and the congregation listened and cried "Yes," "Hallelujah," "Glory," "That's right," and other expressions of appreciation, as if they understood perfectly what he was saying.

I can't pretend that I didn't understand, for it seemed to me that he was simply demonstrating a little more of the mystery of the human being and the human soul. I studied his language, the rhythm and the words, hoping to type them out and to see if I could track them down. They seemed to be rooted in very real languages. From memory I will put down something like what he said: Esposa conta falla almahada appalappa dablu. Said of course with expression, emphasis, and all of the vocal shadings by which spoken words in a sentence take on

93

form. And his own emotional involvement in what he was saying or thinking or communicating rose and fell, so that he was frequently highly excited, that is even more than he was at the outset, even more than anybody in a trance is, and then subsided to more controlled, unemotional, rather intelligent gibberish.

Best of all, though, I went to this church to hear the songs, and to join in the singing: "There is power in the power house." I loved this song because of its proud and loud happiness. And of course there were several songs about being washed in the blood of the lamb.

35. Whitelands House, Kings Road, Chelsea, London, 1966

I TOOK THE 8TH FLOOR FLAT OF SOME LONDON PEOPLE who were visiting members of their family in Australia for three summer months. It was the year 1966. I was 58 years old. My son was 23, my daughter was 20, and I took the place because she was in London, living off the kindness of various friends, the sort of thing that embarrasses me. I told her it was not permissible for her to accept the kindness of friends. She replied that her friends wanted her to occupy one of the many empty rooms in their flats, that they begged her to do so, that she was good company for the head woman of the family, and frequently looked after the kids, if the family had kids, and so on and so forth. I replied that falling into such a pattern was harmful to the character —it was a bad procedure. She could visit her friends briefly, overnight or a weekend, provided she had her own home to visit them from, and to return to. She didn't look at things that way at all, and it doesn't matter why she didn't.

I was in Europe. I had my own place in Paris. I made a special trip to London to see her and to find out what her plans were. She wanted to live in London, and look for work in a play, or a part in a film, as well as modeling jobs.

From the Savoy Hotel I met her daily for a week, and I met some of the people she was staying with—two

95

couples, each with two small kids. When both couples were obliged to leave London and my daughter was thinking about who next to phone for a place to stay, I was overwhelmed by a sense of shame, and profound disappointment and anger. I got in touch with the people who had found flats for the people my daughter had spent time with, and after looking at six or seven places during the next two days, I settled for the flat in Whitelands House. My daughter now had a whole big home to herself, shared by a part of her own family: myself. The rent was high, but it was worth it. And in any case I was gambling every night at Crockford's, and at the Colony Club in Berkeley Square, an area of London that I knew quite well from 1944 when I had been a private in the American Army. And at Eric Steiner's Pair of Shoes. I spent around twenty thousand dollars during the three months I was in London.

About two weeks after we had settled down, my son telephoned from New York and I gathered that he was desperate to get out of his flat in the West Eighties, near Riverside Drive and the Hudson, a flat I had visited several times. I understood his need to break away from there, and so in two days he was installed in the 8th floor flat at Whitelands House, too.

"This is our last chance to talk," I said. "To put it on the line, so I'm available at all hours."

Starting sometimes around nine at night, we talked until almost daybreak. Both of them astonished me by their strange lack of common sense, world awareness, or insight into human meaning, even though both had lived for the most part in New York City, and had gone to the most expensive schools (doesn't mean a thing, of course).

We talked for eight full weeks. And then broke up. Perhaps it helped. I don't know.

36. The Stanley Rose Bookshop, Vine Street near Hollywood, 1932

NEXT DOOR WAS LEVY'S RESTAURANT, WHERE EXCELLENT roastbeef was prepared every day, and across the street on Vine was the Brown Derby, where movie celebrities of all kinds arrived and departed. Also across the street was a tobacco store and horserace book, above which a photographer named Peter Hancock had his studio.

One day in 1932, when I was twenty-four, I was loafing around in the bookshop talking with Stanley, and with friends of his who came to the store to loaf and browse.

John Fante came in and asked for a cigarette, but everybody was all out, so we went across the street and I bought us each a pack, and we lighted up, as the saying is. I had been asked by the photographer Peter Hancock to visit his studio, so he could take a few studio pictures—these are snapshots that are done without snappiness. I was about to go up to the photography studio when I noticed the door at the back of the tobacco shop. Two men came running into the shop, and the man behind the tobacco counter pressed a button that released the door latch, and the men went running into the back room. So I did, too, followed by John Fante.

The place was full of horseplayers and smoke and high tension and a mumble of grumbling voices. I looked up at the entries—Arlington Park in Chicago, I believe it was. And I saw the names of the horses in the next race. I considered them, and I considered the names of the jockeys, and John Fante said, "What are you going to do?"

"Make a bet," I said. "I've only got three dollars and eighty cents to my name. I'll bet the three, and if I lose I'll hitchhike back to San Francisco tomorrow. If I win, I'll stay a while."

In the fourth at Arlington I bet Nankin, and in the fifth I bet Volta Maid, in a parlay, across the board, one dollar each way. Wayne Wright was up on each of them. The bookie clerk scribbled the bet on a slip of paper and handed it to me, and I went out and found the stairway next door to the photography studio of Peter Hancock. John Fante didn't want to come along, because either he owed the photographer a dollar or he hated photographers, but I told him to keep me company and he finally decided that he would.

Peter Hancock was about my age, and we were a couple of years older than John Fante, who was not much more than twenty-one, but had already won the friendship and esteem of H. L. Mencken, who had run two of his short stories about life in an Italian family in Denver in the best magazine in the country, *The American Mercury.*

The photographer set up the right situation, studied the subject, myself, ignored the subject's friend, Fante, who in turn ignored him, although now and then each said something to the other through me, but the things said were both funny and friendly. After a visit of about an hour, the photographer had finished his work, and he said he would have some prints to show me the following day.

"If I'm in town," I said. "If I've lost my bet, I've got to get back to San Francisco."

John Fante and I went down the plain straight-line steps to the street, and into the tobacco shop. The instant I stepped into the betting room I knew each of the two horses had won. Everybody stepped aside, making a path for me to the payoff window. For three dollars I was paid just a few cents under $100.

I loaned Fante three, and Cherry the painter three, and I stayed in town two weeks.

37. Doctor's Office, Oakland, California, 1912

WE MARCHED TO SUNDAY SCHOOL AND CHURCH FROM the Orphanage in Oakland, but one day on our way back, when the formation fell to pieces, I went off to Diamond Canyon to be in the shade of a spot I knew. I looked at the silent fish in the shaded water, and watched the skaters skimming the surface with flawless ease and skill.

When I finally remembered to get along, to the wash-up before Sunday lunch, and left that cool oasis in the world, there was no sign of the other members of the Small Boys' Ward (Mrs. Winchester in charge). Still, I knew my way and was soon at the foot of the steep curved driveway to the entrance. I was climbing up the incline when a boy of ten or eleven on a borrowed bicycle came roaring down the driveway, directly at me. Naturally I jumped to one side, but he in turn steered his bike to the same side, struck me head-on, knocked me down so that my head struck one of the large, jagged rocks that served to mark the line of the flower bed. I was surprised that the collision and the fall were both painless, but I did feel disgraced (removed from the dimension of grace, that is, by the accident, bumped, lifted off my feet, knocked down). When I got to my feet and placed my hand over my left eye because there was a slight condition of discomfort there, and drew my hand away, my hand was covered with blood.

Blood? I thought. This must be serious. And I began to cry, while older boys came to my rescue, as it were. I stopped crying almost instantly, for it was embarrassing. And there was really no need to cry. My brother Henry knocked everybody out of the way, and then my sister Cosette came running from the girls' playground. She dragged me into the Superintendent's office, and said, "Mr. Hagen, my brother has been injured. He must see a doctor immediately."

The kindly Scot looked at the cut over the eye, through the eyebrow, and agreed. There was no car on hand, so he jotted down the name and address of a doctor in Oakland, and my sister took me there by streetcar.

In the meantime the Doctor had been informed by telephone that we were on our way, and so he was waiting for us. I took my hand away from the gauze over my eye, and he very gently cleaned the cut with some cotton moistened with medicine. I then saw him thread a surgical needle, and then he began to sew, while I stood and waited. There were seven or eight stitches in all, and my sister and I went out and got aboard a streetcar and returned to the Orphanage and to the Superintendent's office.

Mr. Hagen looked at the eye, or at any rate at the bandage above the eye, and my sister went back to the girls' side of the establishment and I back to the boys'.

The next day my brother Henry said, "The Doctor phoned Mr. Hagen. He said you're a good boy. Did it hurt?"

"No," I said.

The thing that hurt was the accident itself—the foolishness of it.

I have always hated having foolish things happen to me.

101

38. Raphael Hotel, Paris, 1959

THE BIG MOVIE MAN COMPLAINED OVER COFFEE IN October of 1959 that his last girl just wasn't a star, to which I replied, "That can't possibly be so, since there is nobody who is not a star—the fault is either bad directing or bad writing."

I had written a play for the girl. Then, I had taken a Crime-and-Court story owned by the producer, upon which he had spent a quarter of a million dollars, and for twenty thousand dollars (twenty cents?) I had transformed that absurd and boring story into something at least here and there amusing, which the producer six months later sold to another producer for a good net profit.

The big man was pleased and his stooges said so, but they said he would be much happier if I would do an extra ten days of work on the story, because he felt certain things in it could still be improved. I had just come back from a visit to Portugal and Spain, after the departure of my two kids, who had spent the summer with me, and their going had left me rather sharply alone.

There was nothing for it, and although the idea of working on the absurd story again was distasteful, it seemed to me that it might just impel me to forget the sense of isolation in which I now moved and dwelt, until I might get my bearings and be all right again.

Consequently, I told the giant and his hirelings to find me a place to live and work in and I would see what I could do—free of charge. There was nothing in my deal to compel me to do this extra work.

There happened to be an Automobile Show in Paris at the time, and so there were no rooms at the hotels. The only thing the movie hirelings were able to find was a suite at the Raphael, on Avenue Kleber near the Étoile —very expensive. Even a small room at that hotel, sought out by famous people who did not wish to be disturbed by the press or anybody else, was very expensive.

I said, "Well, it's up to you—if you want me to go to work and that's the only place available, you decide. The La Perouse wants the room I'm presently in, because they let me have it with the understanding that I would leave in two days and it is now six."

After an hour, during which the hirelings tried other hotels, and explained the situation to the big man, they called back, and told me to present myself at the desk at the Raphael—everything was in order. And so I moved the few items I carried around with me out of the small attic room at the La Perouse and traveled a mere two short blocks on foot, and was taken by the assistant manager of the Raphael to a very large suite of rooms on the second floor.

"Who has occupied this place in the past?" I asked.

"Well, actually," the man said, "royalty and such—people with servants."

I went to work in a very small part of the apartment, and in a short time I had it—the work was done, but there was nowhere to go, and the isolation I felt was still overpowering, so I took the story and improved it even further, beyond the expectations of the little man who was the big man. He was thrilled by what I had done, and thanked me. But when I left the hotel I was presented with a bill for $668 for ten days.

Months later the hotel informed me that the bill had not been paid by the producer, who insisted that I must pay it.

I paid it. I'll never be a millionaire, that's all.

39. Breen's, Third Street, San Francisco, 1928

ONE DAY DURING MY LUNCH HOUR FROM THE POSTAL Telegraph Office in the Palace Hotel Building on Market Street, I went loafing down Third Street, past the Examiner Building on Jessie, and came to a place called Breen's, midway between Market and Mission, on another narrow street like Jessie, among hock shops and cheap clothing stores.

Well, it was a bar that served the kind of beer permitted under the law during Prohibition, as well as bitters, which a lot of drinkers knew how to use with other permitted drinks in the making of something they considered intoxicating, or at any rate halfway pleasant. It was also a cafeteria-restaurant, with a chef named Schulotzki, who specialized in simple German fare— pigs' knuckles, sauerkraut, mashed potatoes, sausages and frankfurters. All reasonably priced, as the saying is. The tables were good wood, wiped clean by old men in clean aprons—women were not employed, and almost never did a woman enter the place, to drink or eat. A few nuns came by now and then for money from Bill or Bob Breen, the two brothers who owned and operated the place. Bob was the responsible party. Bill was the one who had been a death-defying alcoholic and had been rescued by his brother, with the help of the Church. There was not an ounce of kindness in either of the men, although they affected warmth and friendship as long as you had money. I know, because I used to roll Twenty-six with Bill Breen up front, where he stood behind a counter on the street, and sold cigars and cigarettes, and kept score for dice-shooters.

I remember standing at the Twenty-six board and rolling against Bill Breen from five o'clock one afternoon until six, a full hour, during which I lost all the money I had in the world, about four dollars, which in those days was a lot of money, and now I didn't even have carfare home. I have never been able to ask anybody for money, but on this occasion, desperate and angry not so much at my bad luck as at my having been hypnotized by the foolish game, and having felt that I *would* win—this has been my story, so to put it, in all of the gambling I have done—that I could win, and that I *would* win. I searched through all of my pockets, while Bill Breen watched, but I hadn't a penny left and he knew it. He dropped the pencil he kept ready for the keeping of the score on the pad, and I felt he was going to slip me a silver dollar, but he just looked out into space, or out at the stumblebums moving up and down Third Street.

At last I forced myself to say, "I guess I lost every nickel I have. I haven't even got carfare home."

He just kept looking out into space, and acting as if he were deaf. He died, poor bastard, a good Catholic, a cured alcoholic, and a damned fool. So did Bob—but the place is still there.

In the back, taking up the greater part of the space of the place, were a dozen round tables at which rummy was played, for house chips. If you had a lot of nerve and no money, you could sit in a game and not pay anything and perhaps win something—I did it many times.

Breen's was another of the many foolish places I went to instead of to College.

Was it just as well?

It was better, I believe, but I wouldn't ask anybody else to try it.

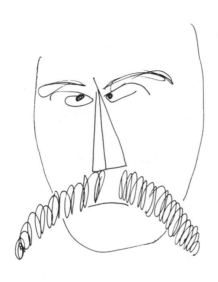

40. Reforma Hotel, Mexico City, 1935

PRUNING MUSCAT VINES ON THE 160-ACRE VINEYARD ON Shields Avenue off Academy, north of the town of Sanger, California—an area of great significance in my life: my father worked for Droge on his vineyard when I was born in 1908, and it was not far from Droge's vineyard that I worked in 1924, in January, thirteen years after my father's death. Pruning vines, I picked up a little Spanish from the Mexicans doing the same work, so that we were able to carry on simple conversations.

Naturally, I wanted to know more about Mexico, so I borrowed a book from the Public Library by Carlton Beals. The book was fascinating, as of course any book about any people would have to be. Still, I especially liked my fellow workers, and I became so interested in Mexico itself that I made up my mind to go there on a visit as soon as possible. I was sixteen years old, and it was not until ten or eleven years later that I actually went there. (I had visited Tia Juana, just across the California state line, but I didn't think of Tia Juana as a real part of Mexico.)

I took a train to Mexico from San Francisco in 1935. It was chair car all the way, the Southern Pacific to Nogales, and a Mexican train from that point on— destination Mexico City. On board the train was an old American prospector and all-around adventurer who had lived in Mexico more than forty of his sixty-five years. I remember one thing he told me, because it struck me as being very wise. He deliberately cultivated a reputation for never being armed—by concealed pistol or knife. This meant that in disputes he could hold to the truth quietly and calmly, and not excite his honest opponents or permit his dishonest ones to shoot him and claim it had been in self-defense.

I found the country profoundly attractive and different—even from the nearby border lands of the United States. One can seldom look at terrain and think of it, "This is France," for instance, but in looking at the landscape south of Nogales I had the feeling unmistakably. The land itself was Mexican. It was dry, sandy, rocky, hot, and heavy with many kinds of desert plants. It had repose, dignity, and a sense of the fierceness of survival—not just human survival, but *all* survival, animal, insect, bird, and plant. And then, when the people of Mexico appeared beyond the train windows, this isolation, struggle, and heroism was clearly marked in their faces.

In Mexico City I went to the newest and best hotel, the Reforma, because wasn't I a writer, a man who made rather good money from very easy work which he would have done even if he hadn't been able to earn any money from it?

I felt hushed by the poverty, patience, dignity, and even seeming backwardness of the Mexican people, even in the big city. I walked everywhere and I looked at everything and everybody.

One Saturday night in a bar everything was so explosive, hot, secret, and irrepressible, I wondered there wasn't even more violence among the murmuring, milling crowd of surely more than two hundred men and women where just the night before two men had died of knife wounds, after an argument.

41. 2729 West Griffith Way, Fresno, California, 1964

IN 1963 I HAD DONE A LOT OF LIVING AND TRAVELING, AND I thought it would be pleasant to go back to my hometown, my birthplace, Fresno, and feel some of the summertime ease I had felt when I had been there long ago, from 1915 to 1926, in fact—ten years of very great importance in my life.

I drove down from San Francisco in a little red Karmann-Ghia I had bought in 1959 in Belgrade, and I parked the car just a little outside the heart of town. I walked and looked at places I hadn't looked at in many years. I didn't go to a hotel or motel, because I wasn't sure I wanted to hang around longer than an hour or two. I saw some faces I had known in the past but not well enough to remember the name of the person attached to the face, except to think, "Armenian. Italian. Portuguese. American. Slovenian. Syrian. Assyrian." And so on.

I looked into places on Broadway, and sure enough little illegal card-games were still going on, most of the players Armenians under the age of thirty—or should I say under the age of eighty? (That would be more like it, although most of the players *were* under thirty.) It was very hot. I found a place with rootbeer on tap.

There were bees flying around and lighting on the spigot of the big barrel from which the rootbeer was drawn. And that did it.

The flavor of the cool, foamy rootbeer did it, or at any rate made me decide that this heat was mine and I had better have some of it again. I walked back to my car, drove to the Californian Hotel, and took a room on the 8th floor, overlooking old Armenian Town, long since shot, almost all finished. I then went out to examine the whole town some more, and the next day I drove out to the old and new residential areas, to see what they looked like.

North of the famous old Roeding Park just off Highway 99 I came to a small tract of houses—brandnew and cheap. I decided to have a look at them, so I stopped, and a big overgrown boy with a Lithuanian name took me around to see the various houses, some finished, some almost finished, some half-finished, and quite a few just started.

"This house is thirteen five," he said, which meant the price was thirteen thousand five hundred, on a corner, across from a vineyard.

"What about that vineyard over there?" I said.

"They want too much money," the salesman said. "They won't sell. They're rich, anyway. I guess the vineyard will stay there for ten years or more, but sooner or later it has got to go."

I went through the house and liked it, all empty. I bought the house, and two weeks later when I drove down from San Francisco and moved in the place was mine.

The house next door seemed to have a good floor plan, so I bought it, too. Now, whenever I get to California from my home in Paris, I drive to my houses in Fresno, across from the vineyard, and I loaf around and let time do what it must to everything and everybody.

42. Fresno, 1926

THE FIRST PURPOSE OF MY LIFE AFTER I REACHED THE
age of ten or eleven was to get away from Fresno as
soon as possible. It was a great place to look back on
and remember perhaps, but of course no man knows
such a thing when he's there in the middle of it. The
fact is the only reason it was ever a great place was myself, my *saying* so. In itself it was a lively if poor and
stupid place, although there were some people who were
not exactly poor in possessions and some others who
were not exactly backward in the dimension of clever-
ness. Otherwise it was a place to avoid, and if that was
not possible, to get away from as soon as possible.

Going away has something to do with the search in
general—for love, for the beautiful girl or woman who
is to fulfill a man's truth and reality, for recognition, for
acceptance, for work, for enthusiasm about the whole
human experience, but most of all going away is a
search for one's best self. It is not just simply getting
up and going. It is also the beginning of the embrac-
ing of the whole world, of putting one's arms around
it and holding it in a tight and loving embrace. It is a
moving out to all of the human race, not just that portion of it that happens to be where a man happens to
be—held prisoner, as he sometimes feels. Mainly, in
spite of the terrible boredom and stupidity and mean-
ness of Fresno, my life there was full of drama and swift

growth. Being in the streets from the beginning and going to all of the places of the city and seeing all of the members of the human race there, I found more than enough to keep my mind and soul fully occupied.

Everything was all right, one might say, except that there was more wrong with every part of everything than right. Much more.

I began to leave in 1926, when I was pretty well along in years, almost eighteen, after having had a full decade of important growth in the busy town. I was gone for good (or at any rate almost for good) by the time I was nineteen. Thereafter I went back for a visit now and then, but these visits were very brief, and their purpose was to check various places and people, and to confirm certain facts or truths.

San Francisco was the place that followed Fresno, and it was a whole new world, with a far better location, climate, culture, and humanity. But I traveled from San Francisco, too. I had to see everything, or as much of everything as I could possibly manage with the money I earned, or won at gambling, or acquired from the faithful cultivation of my skill as a writer—and from the hard work of writing.

Going away, going to a new place, was beautiful. It pleased me in a way that very nearly nothing else could please me. It was a large act of pure love.

43. Savoy Hotel, London, 1935

THE STRAND BEGAN TO FEEL LIKE HOME TO ME WHEN I first found it on a short visit to London in 1935, on my way to Russia for the first time, on my first visit to Europe itself. Covent Garden, just up a bit, with its sweet smells of fresh produce of all kinds, its noise and action, always drew me away from the Strand for a half-hour of loitering and breathing deeply of the scent of good leafery of all kinds, stalks, berries, melons, and all of the other good things that were in season. Charing Cross, with its grand Hotel and the fine pedestal and sculpture out front (I once waited an hour for some kind of bird to alight on it, but none did. The figure didn't scare them away, but something about the monument seemed to keep them at a distance.) Trafalgar Square, the beautiful church, St. Martin's, the British Museum, and all the rest of it. But the heart of the Strand to me was from Charing Cross to Waterloo Bridge—and there, the entrance almost concealed, was the Savoy Hotel.

It was inevitable that as soon as possible, as soon as I could afford it, I would stop there. On that first visit to London I could not afford it, of course. I was traveling everywhere on very little money, and I took the rooms and meals and trains and ships that were indicated in the deal. It was the first large travel, the first overseas. It was a break-through. It was as great an achievement as the publication of my first book. The hotel I was booked into was not far from Russell Square, where Faber & Faber had their establishment. The hotel was on a desolate street down which hawkers strolled and made their rather beautiful street cries, especially an old woman who had roses to sell. The hotel had no name, or certainly its name was irrelevant: bed and breakfast for under the equivalent of one dollar, something like that.

But in 1939 I began to go to the Savoy, where I was happy to pay the tariff—about six dollars a day at the beginning, until now, in 1969, it is about four times as much, certainly never under twenty dollars a day. I really hadn't known that the Savoy was a very famous place. I had just liked the Strand, and I had wanted to be there.

When I was a private in the U.S. Army, stationed in London in 1944, I was permitted to stay at the Savoy, by special dispensation, but at my own expense, in order to be able to work at the writing of a novel likely to enhance cordial Anglo-American relations, but at the same time, for myself, more fully and meaningfully a novel that was against war—for any reason. Through a man named Herbert Agar, once of Kentucky but lately a Londoner, high in war-time political importance, both with the Embassy and with the Office of War Information, an understanding was reached between himself and myself, between the U.S. Government and a citizen, between the Army and a private: for the writing of a novel, I would be granted a special leave during which I would be permitted to visit my wife and young son in New York.

And so I took up residence at the Savoy, room 360, which looked down on a narrow alley to the Strand, where I could see people walking the width of the alley.

I worked like a maniac, and in 38 days wrote a novel called *The Adventures of Wesley Jackson*. The work nearly killed me, but Herbert Agar, the Government, and the Army welshed.

The OWI went dead and refused either to arrange for my leave (although other privates in my outfit, with good connections with Hollywood Majors and Colonels, were flying to New York virtually at will), or even to let me know the status of the manuscript. At least one Hollywood Major (a very bad writer) got hold of the manuscript by trickery and reported to various Army agencies and to the OWI that the book must not be published, and furthermore that the author ought to be shot. Actual publication by Harcourt, Brace was in fact delayed even after the war ended.

Why was this so?

The book was anti-dishonesty, and only incidentally anti-war. It was more pro the enemy than anti for the simple reason that the very term enemy is dishonest.

That's why.

44. The Hampshire House, New York, 1939

THE YEAR 1939 WAS A BIG IF TERRIBLE YEAR FOR THE world, but especially for the Western world. I arrived in the American theatre with two plays, *My Heart's in the Highlands* in April, and *The Time of Your Life* in October.

The German Army walked into Poland on September 1st, the day after my 31st birthday, and the War was on.

But who can experience the agony of others? Who can experience another man's truth?

From The Great Northern Hotel on West 57th Street I moved two blocks to the Hampshire House, on Central Park South. My large room with grand bath, hall, and serving pantry overlooked Central Park, from the 28th floor, and I felt like a Lord. I didn't need to think about money at all, and if I *did* think about it, it was in connection with the other members of my immediate family. I had already bought a house in a big, new hillside development in San Francisco, in the Sunset District, early in 1939, while the house was still on paper. I asked Henry Doelger, the builder, to take advantage of the third level, and to fix me up a good apartment down there. The rest of the house was for my mother Takoohi, and for my sister Cosette.

While the house was being completed, I traveled to Mexico, then to New York, then to Europe—London,

Paris, and Dublin—then back to New York, back to San Francisco, to visit the new house for the first time, to begin trying out the new apartment, for size, as it were.

While in the new apartment, for about a month, I tried writing there. I had become fond of writing in the front room at 348 Carl Street, and when I first saw the new apartment I disliked it. The sun reached it only in the late afternoon, not in the morning, as it had on Carl Street, and I felt I wouldn't want to try to work in this new, sunless place. But the fireplace took the place of the sun, and I *did* work. I wrote *Sweeney in the Trees,* and then *Love's Old Sweet Song,* and several shorter plays. Then, I returned to New York, and moved into the Hampshire House.

Besides all the travel, and all the work, there was always a great deal of eating, drinking, and fooling around. Girls and women were abundant, and with enough alcohol down the gullet selectivity was put off until next time. But I did draw the line on a girl who took the service stairs at the Hampshire House, climbed 28 floors, rested, rang the doorbell, and was asked by me to come in. She was a large girl, obviously repressed, terribly excitable, and not quite right. After chatting with her for half an hour or so, during which I took her a drink of Scotch to see if that might calm her—she didn't want it, so I drank it myself—it turned out that she had spent a year in a public hospital for the mentally disturbed, she was from a very poor family who lived somewhere in the Bronx, she had planned on meeting me for a week, she had been afraid to present herself to the Desk. Physically, she was desirable—large, full, well made. But I knew it wouldn't do.

118

When she was relaxed and felt that we had become friends, I asked her if there was anything I could do, and she said, "Yes, one thing. Please take me down by elevator, and walk out with me." I did that, and then took her to Rumpelmayer's for some refreshment for herself, and coffee for me, and then I made her take twenty dollars, so that she could at least get home by taxi.

And I drew the line with a very attractive movie star who suggested sixty-nine, and couldn't believe I didn't understand what she meant. It was a very exciting personal time, a very sad world time, and although I was famous and rich at last, I knew it really didn't mean anything.

45. Ahboud's Stand at the Fresno Free Market, 1917

WHEN I WAS NINE OR TEN I BEGAN TO TAKE SATURDAY morning jobs at the Free Market at the north end of the Court House Park, a long line of small fruit and vegetable stands.

One Saturday I went up to a dark little man and asked if he wanted somebody to help him. By way of reply he gestured that I might lift the other end of the board, so that he could proceed with the assembling of his stand. In short, I was hired.

On previous Saturdays for a month I had worked for Long John, a very tall and loud Armenian who paid me half a dollar for work from six in the morning until two in the afternoon, at which time the stands were broken down and the small merchants went home. Half a dollar was better than nothing of course, and I was happy to have it, and to do my work well, but on this particular morning I decided to try somebody else. The dark little man and I did not discuss wages, because it wasn't done in those days. A boy wanted work, a man gave him work. At the end of the workday the man paid him, the boy accepted the pay. The following Saturday he returned or not, and the man hired him again or not. It was all free and easy, entirely voluntary on all sides, but as long as a boy was at work he was expected to work.

I heard a number of people refer to this new man by the name of Ahboud, and I heard him exchange a few words with them—in a language I did not know. It was Syrian or Lebanese, with a variety of gutturals in it.

After we had set up the stand, and had put boxes of fruit and vegetables on display, Ahboud handed me a cloth and asked me to shine the oranges. He watched me quickly transform a dusty orange into a sparkling jewel, nodded, and himself worked at more difficult or complicated problems—he had six boxes of tomatoes in which some were becoming oversoft. These he carefully removed to a separate box, and later offered them to some old ladies who came by, for almost nothing—six or seven pounds for a nickel, for instance. They knew what to do with such tomatoes. They knew that such tomatoes were the best for their purposes. They made a concentrate of them, called salsa, which served them during the winter.

When the shoppers began to arrive at the free market, Ahboud and everybody else began to lift his voice, calling attention to the beautiful stuff he had for sale, and to the bargain prices. He didn't need to tell me to do the same, I did it on my own, and began to sell new figs, apricots, peaches, oranges, okra, string beans, tomatoes, and all sorts of other good things. Ahboud dropped a watermelon around eight o'clock in the morning and invited me to share the heart with him. It was delicious. At ten he found a casaba with a big crack in it, so he broke it open at the crack, and gave me half, and a knife, and again I feasted. The other stuff I didn't touch—not even a cherry. I knew he was a good man, and I had no intention of taking advantage of him. By noon we had sold almost everything. At two when the stand was dismantled and back in place on his wagon, he reached into his pocket, full of coins, and brought out a silver dollar. He handed it to me, nodded, and I went home. The next Saturday I was back at half past five, and I worked again with Ahboud. He was a good guy. He sold good stuff.

46. The Gilbert Hotel, Hollywood, 1933

JIM TULLY WAS AT THE MARK TWAIN HOTEL, JUST UP from the Gilbert Hotel where I was stopping. He had a fine home somewhere in the hills, but he rented a room at the Mark Twain and went there every day to put in a little time writing, or maybe to lie on the bed and sleep. It is sad that almost nobody knows who Jim Tully was. He was a writer, from somewhere in Ohio, and he went out to Hollywood as a young man, after a number of years on the railroads of the country—a hobo. One might say a professional hobo. He was short, thick, broad-shouldered, and he had very red abundant hair, and very small hands and feet. Ilya Ehrenburg in Paris in 1966 at a big public event on behalf of something or other righteous made an impassioned speech from the platform, standing behind a lectern, but when he came down the main aisle after the meeting I noticed that he was a larger man than Jim Tully but that he had hands and feet that were possibly even smaller than Jim Tully's. They are both dead, Jim Tully twenty years or more, and Ilya Ehrenburg two or three. Ehrenburg went through a lot of history and managed to survive the malicious mysteries and murders of the Stalin regime in Russia, while his friend Isaac Babel did not. And the big thing about Ehrenburg's achievement is that he was a man of art, an intellectual, and at heart a European.

He was also honest, but obviously he knew how to keep his honesty in check at the proper time. His autobiography (in four volumes) is a document of special interest for many reasons. Jim Tully on the other hand was not involved in anything historical at any time—he did not rush over to Spain at the time of the Civil War, as Mr. Ernest Hemingway did, for instance. He just stayed in Hollywood and spent quite a lot of time at the Mark Twain Hotel.

I took a room at the Gilbert Hotel a block down on the same street because it was a less depressing place and the rent was about the same—two or three dollars a day, or about fourteen dollars by the week. My visits were not prolonged, but almost invariably I ran into Jim Tully coming out of or going into the Mark Twain Hotel, and we would stop and talk a minute or two. Sometimes Jim Tully would get going and he would keep going and soon we would be in one or another of the good beer joints on Hollywood Boulevard and he would be telling me how he had started a whole school of American writing, which Mr. Ernest Hemingway had come along and taken credit for.

"The short staccato sentence," Jim Tully said with annoyance, "was my discovery. I used it in my articles in *Vanity Fair* and in three novels before Hemingway was published, even."

Jim Tully never suspected that it may not have been the short staccato sentence that was at the bottom of Mr. Hemingway's great appeal, not just to English-speaking peoples, but to readers all over the world. And then a little later Jim Tully bitterly cursed Charlie Chaplin.

124

"I worked for him a year, and he used my stuff, but

he didn't pay me a dime. He really thinks it's enough for writers to be permitted to know him."

And then, "Right over there at that table, John Gilbert came over to let me know he didn't like what I had written about him in *Vanity Fair,* but I had written the truth, so I hit him over the head with the beer bottle beside my glass—but lightly, otherwise I might have killed him."

He knew everybody in Hollywood well enough to despise them.

At the Gilbert Hotel, a published writer at last, I marveled how much like everybody else the writers were that I knew: Jo Pagano, Owen Francis, John Fante, Horace McCoy, and a good dozen or more others. One of them published one book and disappeared: William Rollins, Jr.

47. Room on 43rd Street
near 7th Avenue, New York, 1928

IN NEW YORK I MOVED FROM ONE ROOM TO ANOTHER, both in order to know various parts of town a little more fully than if I had only walked by and because every room I occupied wasn't really fit for human habitation but would do for two or three nights. My days were long and the nights were short, and the rooms were only places to sleep in anyhow. I got up at five every morning to take the subway to City Hall, from whence I walked four or five blocks to the Postal Telegraph Office in Washington Market, among the wholesale produce houses, at number 120 Warren Street. I was off duty at three in the afternoon, whereupon I continued my explorations of Manhattan, Brooklyn, Coney Island, Jersey, and other places accessible by subway or by other inexpensive transportation, like the ferry-boat rides for a nickel—to Jersey, to Staten Island, and so on.

I took a room at a three-story rooming house on 43rd Street near Seventh Avenue, but it was an inside room, without a window. The lighting was by gas jet. There was always a smell of gas in the whole building. I stayed in this place about a week because of the location, in the very heart of Manhattan, but finally I had to move on. Across the street was a big electric sign that went on and off as soon as dark of night arrived: Joe Cook in *Rain or Shine*. I never saw that musical comedy, although I knew Joe Cook was a very funny fellow. When I arrived in New York in August *Rain or Shine* was a hit, and when I left in January it was still running, but to this day I don't know what kind of a show it was.

I paid money to see *Strange Interlude* at a theatre on 59th Street. Standing room fifty cents, a big important cast, the most important American playwright, and I kept swearing I could write better (as of course I could).

And then one night I went out of my way to get to a theatre where a new play had arrived, which according to the *Times* didn't look as if it was going to hang around very long. *Congai* was the name of the play, and the reason I hurried around to see it was that the play had been staged by Rouben Mamoulian, and I knew that anybody with a name like that came from Armenia. The play was in fact magnificently staged—which was the best thing about it. I didn't meet the director, and of course I didn't try to meet him—what would I have said to him? And then I paid another half-dollar to see a play starring Osgood Perkins. It was called *Ceiling Zero,* and was full of the spurious excitement which so many American plays of that time thrived on. There was an explosion in the third act, for instance, that shook the whole theatre and scared the shit out of everybody. That alone may have made the play a big success. And finally I paid another half-dollar to stand at the back of a theatre to see Lew Leslie's *Blackbirds of 1928,* which I liked best of all—because the people were black, the girls very pretty, the men very funny, and the whole show high-spirited. To this day I continue to sing the big song of that show: *I Can't Give You Anything but Love, Baby.*

127

But the main theatre in New York for me was The Palace, because vaudeville was my home, as it had been in Fresno and in San Francisco. I needed variety, and it was only in vaudeville that I was sure of getting it.

The reason I left the gaslit room was that the gas leaked one night so badly that the landlady had to come to the room to shut it off properly.

48. Bucharest Hotel, Moscow, 1935

THE FIRST FAR TRAVEL IS MOST DEEPLY MEANINGFUL, especially if the traveler is not a child and has earned his passage and paid for it out of his own pocket, time, and life. That is how it was with me at the age of 27, when I went to Europe and to Soviet Russia.

Traveling as inexpensively as possible, I stopped at hotels that were not high class, as one has a right to say, even in Russia, but to me were nevertheless rather grand. I certainly had a nice room on the highest floor of the Bucharest Hotel in Moscow in June of 1935, and a bath down the hall, and good Russian food. I was writing a short story every day during my travels in Russia, and I didn't want being in Moscow to interrupt this program. Having arrived in the early afternoon and having wanted to get out into the city to see the sights, I got the day's story out of the way in a matter of something well under an hour, and then I was free to get out and be a tourist—the Intourist guide was a young girl who spoke the odd kind of meticulous incorrect English that all such people speak, and after about an hour in Red Square just across the Moscow River, and a look at Lenin in his tomb, I told the girl I was going back to the hotel for a nap, and so we agreed to meet early the following morning, when she would take me to see New Kindergartens. This permitted me to wander around Moscow in my own manner and at my own convenience. Here and there I got the impression that I was out of bounds, and now and then a young cop told me so in Russian. There was no real system or sense to what was out of bounds and what wasn't. I had a nice day, and in the evening I went to a theatre and saw something musical and bright that made me so happy I kept laughing, which compelled people to turn and look at me. Laughing is not frowned upon in Russia alone. Years later, at a performance of James Thurber's *The Male Animal*, the comedy affected me so powerfully that an usher was sent to ask me not to laugh so loudly, I was disturbing the rest of the audience. That's life, as they say, that's Russia, that's Broadway, that's people, that's me. The play in Moscow turned out to be *The Bat*—that's all, but in Russian the word was *The Flying-Mouse*. I couldn't have had a nicer time.

Back at the Bucharest Hotel I went to the dining room for supper, around eleven at night, and people were just beginning to settle down for the evening meal. Another difference. This was not an after-theatre snack, it was dinner. Many Russians ate dinner at two in the morning, I was informed later. The meal was quite nice, if slowly and poorly served: caviar, borscht, woodcock, and compote. There was always compote at the end of a meal, and quite frequently caviar at the start.

I felt that I was in a world that was different, but not really strange, and I considered everybody a friend.

One morning outside the Bucharest Hotel I chatted with an American who turned out to be William Z. Foster, the candidate for President on the Communist ticket several times. He was sick with despair because Stalin had starved twenty million peasants to death—as punishment for not handing over all of their crops and livestock to the Party. Two slick young New York college boys sneered at my writing, which they had not read, in comparison with Jack London's, who was a favorite of theirs and of millions of Russians, and a favorite of mine, as well. They were obviously rich sons of bitches, and very Communistic in a snide way.

The second day in Moscow, I went to work on a story that kept going for more than four solid hours: *Moscow in Tears,* because of the rain. The manager of the hotel said he would mail it for me, I believed him, he did not mail it, and it is still lost.

49. Athenee Palace Hotel, Bucharest, Romania, 1969

In May of 1969 I decided to travel from my home at 74 Rue Taitbout in Paris to Vienna, and from there to sail the Danube to Odessa on the Black Sea, for I had been to Odessa in 1960 and had loved the place, especially the Jewish cemetery, and the Synagogue, which was actually a large, barnlike building. I wanted to wander around in the streets again, along the waterfront, up on the high embankment, and out to the little neighborhoods which I imagined Isaac Babel had noticed when he had been a kid in Odessa. And I wanted to go to the Opera again, and to think about the great numbers of concert musicians born and brought up in Odessa—but apparently not one composer. My longing to see Odessa was eager, but something happened.

The Russian Consul in Paris sent back my passport to the travel agency and said it had expired. I walked four miles in a hurry to the travel agency, to the American Embassy, where I was informed that the passport was valid for six more months, and then to the Russian Consul, who had shut his doors for the day. Somebody left the building, so I went in before the door became latched shut. I was pretty hot and didn't mind letting the Consul and his staff know what I thought of them. Wasn't it enough that they interpreted the rules and regulations of Russia? Did they believe they had to interpret those of the United States, too? The Consul came running to say, "Your visa is ready, your visa is ready."

I felt, "Sure it's ready, you mother. But it should have been ready ten days ago, in a very simple routine way."

To the man I said, "You use it, I'm not going. Just give me back the three photographs I provided."

And I walked home, thinking, "You're getting too hot. If you expect to travel, you have got to expect Consuls all over the world to be at least *stupid*."

Thus, the visit to Odessa was spoiled. From Odessa I had planned to fly to Erivan, and that also was spoiled. I just didn't like the idea of not being able to get a visa in a routine way. I didn't like the production that was made of granting it.

But the idea of sailing down the Danube was still a good idea, so I flew to Vienna, and looked into sailings.

I booked a cabin on the Russian ship for the next sailing, in three days, and had short but pleasant visits in Bratislava, Budapest, Belgrade, and Russe. The final port for me was just across the Danube from Russe, the town of Giurgiu, Romania, from whence I traveled by bus fifty miles north to Bucharest, where I presented myself to the Desk at the Athenee Palace Hotel, because I had read in a brochure that it was the best hotel in town.

It was, but the Manager insisted he had no room, not one. The lobby was full of delegates from all over the world to various conventions, so I had every reason to believe him.

I took a chance and remarked that I was an American writer, my stuff had been translated into the Romanian language, and my plays had been performed on the stages of Bucharest, whereupon three of the desk clerks began fishing around in their records and charts. They chatted with the Manager, and finally I got a room that was great.

After I had settled down I began to think, "Hell, I went to a hotel called Bucharest, in Moscow, in 1935, precisely 34 years ago. The Manager of the Bucharest lied to me, he was a spy, he didn't mail my story to New York, he stole it, and now he's dead, the records are all shot, perhaps the story is lost forever, or even destroyed. Well, forget it, forget it, plenty more where that came from."

But it's not so at all. *Moscow in Tears* is the only one of its kind.

50. 40 West 58th Street, New York, 1948

HAVING A WIFE AND TWO KIDS TO MAINTAIN, AT THE same time that writing must be done (or there won't be anything to maintain anybody *with*) is not an easy job. If the little woman, who kept crying before she became the little bride, swearing devotion and all of the other wifely things, is unhappy where she is and must be diverted every fifteen minutes, or must be moved into a new place in which to be unhappy, and to make phone calls all day and all night—her mother said her bones were strong, she didn't say anything about her real charms, her hilarious untidiness if she didn't have somebody do everything for her, or her continuous sickness if she wasn't on the phone or giving a party or buying clothes for herself. If the little woman isn't with it, having other ideas, values, and purposes, the going is bound to be just a little rough on the laughing, inexhaustible boyo who is the lucky husband. He is going to do a lot of drinking, just to dull the disbelief about the bargain he got, and then he is going to try to guess if there might be some way to get something out of the bargain, and he is going to discover that there is, the oldest bargain of them all, on an average of once a night, but sometimes twice, and now and then three times.

135

"We've got to get away from here," the little bride said at three one morning. "Let me tell my mother to go ahead and find an apartment in New York. San Francisco is for the birds. Let me tell her. Please. Let me phone her and tell her. Please."

The next morning, or at any rate four hours later, the lucky husband went to work and tried to write something, but the stuff just wasn't any good, he was too shot, too confused, too tired, too dried out, too juiceless, too alone—in spite of his bed pal, in spite of his two kids, in spite of the series of crazy women who were hired to look after them. At two in the afternoon, looking like the woman taken in adultery in a Cecil B. De Mille Bible movie, she cried, "Oh, darling, mother has found the most wonderful brandnew apartment in the heart of New York and the rent's very cheap, only $500 a month, unfurnished. My God, we'll feel alive again, we'll feel back in civilization again, this is no life."

It seems her mother and she had been talking on the phone for days and her mother had found the place a week ago but the daughter had wanted to wait for the best possible moment to break the news.

And so there was nothing for it. They moved from San Francisco to the 2nd floor, dreary little stupid apartment in New York, but of course it didn't help—the little bride was still miserable if she had to do anything for herself, and she became desperately sick if she wasn't at a party, or giving one.

I thought it was great. It seemed to me as good a way as any to commit suicide. If everything had been done to make her happy and comfortable and rich and well-fed and well-rested and amused—why, this little girl was really quite a friend, quite a nice little friend. And a man thanked God for her little mother.

51. 24848 Malibu Road, Malibu, California, 1951

SUICIDE WAS SUICIDE, DIVORCE WAS DIVORCE. I FLIPPED A coin, and it came up divorce. The *second* divorce, that is, from the same little bride. I was bankrupt, in debt to the Tax Collector for about fifty thousand dollars, about half that much to others, most of them merchants who had sold her stuff. During the short second marriage I had bought her diamond rings, fancy dentistry, expensive furs, shoes and clothes. This hungry little girl with the pudgy, spongy flesh at which she worked better than half the day in order to be ready in the evening for her public at another party talked and laughed, and talked and laughed, and talked and laughed, and consulted her lawyer. She was a real Broadway musical comedy. Everybody loved her, men and women alike.

Her lawyer was the most famous in Beverly Hills, who imagined he was among the immortals of law. My lawyer had been recommended by a man I had considered a friend. In going over the papers, however, I noticed that the little woman had agreed to find an apartment to rent somewhere, for herself and the two kids, with a rent not to exceed a hundred dollars a month. Well, there just wasn't any such apartment unless you went to the slums. I didn't like the idea of the kids' being in such a place.

I said, "No, I don't want that. I'll find a new house

somewhere, I'll make the down payment, and I'll make the monthly payments."

My lawyer protested and said if I insisted on such a thing he would leave the case immediately.

This annoyed me, so I told him to leave.

He did, and sued me and collected a couple of thousand dollars for his fee.

In the end I got them into a fine house in Pacific Palisades, and I looked around for a place for myself. At last on the Beach at Malibu I found a little house on top of piling, and I bought some basic furniture and moved in. It was 1951. I was forty-three years old. I was very tired. I was very broke. I was very mad, but in that house on the Beach I had the feeling that I was home, I was back in the world of the spirit, the world of truth, and I began to get back my soul.

But how could I, how could I *ever*, how could I *permit* myself to actually get up and leave such a joyous, luminous treasure of a girl? Well, I really don't know how. Just more of my stupidity, I guess. Just more of the same unfortunate behavior that put me to marrying her in the first place—taking her away from the world, to have all to myself. That's not right. I was punished for doing such a selfish thing. My punishment was the divorce and my arrival in the house on the Beach.

52. Attic Room, Fred Finch Orphanage, Oakland, 1912

I WAS PUT INTO THE ATTIC ROOM IN CASE MY ILLNESS WAS contagious. Whatever it was, it was murder. I was four years old, and I had long since reasoned that it was folly to expect the big things from people. It was enough to get the little ones. The biggest thing of course was love, the nearness of somebody you love when you *need* somebody to be near. And I needed somebody then, Christmas Eve.

A fever raged in my bones, but I didn't know it was a fever. I only knew that something inside was trying to burn me up and tear me to pieces. And I knew I needed help. The best help would be from the great one, the Mother. I imagined she would somehow know I was fighting a very hard fight and would hurry from Laguna Street in San Francisco by ferry boat to Oakland and come up the stairs and open the door—and there she would be. But after a long time, when the door opened, it was a strange woman with a strange smell who was assigned to look in on me now and then. She didn't speak. She just presented herself, looked at me, and went away. And again I began to imagine the great one would open the door and come in. It was night, something was going on inside me that I couldn't do anything to stop, except wait, but the waiting was very hard to do.

Suddenly I heard the voices of the kids at the Orphanage singing a song that has never ceased to mean many strange things to me: *O Holy Night*. The song and the voices were so beautiful it was all I could do not to die—not to escape into the sorrow they spoke of and were. But I refused. I was alone, and it would never be known that I cried, but I refused. For I did not feel I was really alone as long as *I* was there. I was still there, changed, in trouble, burning, desperate, but I was still myself, and I lived by the law and preference that I would look after myself.

I listened to the kids singing and waited eagerly for their return to the part in which they cried out, *Fall on your knees, O hear the angel voices.*

I saw the human race, inside itself, everywhere, fall on its knees, and listen. The angel voices were the kids singing of course, and I not only listened, I found a moment of new pride and peace in doing so, but I did not fall on my knees. (We kneeled at our beds in silent prayer every night, but when I had been taken to the attic room and had kneeled at the bed the woman had said, "It's all right. Just get in bed.)

That night was one of the longest I have ever lived through. I might have died. I knew something deadly wrong had happened to me, but at that time I did not believe, I refused to believe, that anything could kill me. At the same time I knew everything could, anything could—it happened every day, and it could happen to me—but I refused to believe that it could or would. It was just that the loneliness was so killing, even while you stood your ground, and refused. If the great one found out about my fight with Death and came to be near me, then, what good things we might all expect from being in the world.

I fell into delirious, painful sleep but hated it so deeply that I woke up almost instantly and waited awake, and then around daybreak I knew I had come through, and now at last fell into real sleep—alone, and proud, and alive—now more alive than ever.

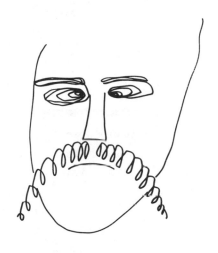

'

53. The Panama Pacific International Exposition, San Francisco, 1915

THE EIGHT BOYS OF THE WARD FOR SMALL BOYS WERE taken by streetcar and ferry boat by Blanche Fulton to the Fair in San Francisco. We were supremely well-behaved, not because we enjoyed being well-behaved but because it was part of our agreement with Blanche Fulton. She told us quite plainly that she could manage eight small boys at a World's Fair only if they were well-behaved, and we instantly agreed that we would do only that which she asked us to do, and nothing else. And we didn't break our word. Blanche Fulton took pride in us that whole day. Our clothes were all freshly cleaned and ironed, put on after we had had baths that morning. Every boy presented a picture of a healthy, clean, well-dressed, serious-minded inmate of an orphanage, but of course we didn't think of ourselves in that way at all. The fact is we didn't think of ourselves at all, we thought of the Fair, the wonders ahead. The whole day was to be spent at the Fair, and Miss Fulton, out of her own generous pocket and heart, was going to treat us to a good lunch, and to some of the other refreshments we might see and need. She was a rare old maid. Unpaid volunteer, she achieved more important things on behalf of the kids than any of the other people at the Orphanage. What's more, she liked the kids. She spoke to them by name, and with obvious love, or the disappointment of one whose love has been betrayed.

Four on one side of her, four on the other, we strolled about the Fair. Suddenly from around a magnificent oriental building two camels appeared, followed by four Arabs in colorful costumes. One of them was making strange music on a pipe of some kind. I was so surprised and delighted that the image and sound have stayed with me ever since. We saw an airplane flying very low over the waters of the Golden Gate, and then we saw it quickly rise high and begin to do what was then called a loop-the-loop. We saw shining, almost imaginary buildings, full of unbelievable works of sculpture, painting, weaving, basketmaking, products of agriculture, and all kinds of mechanical inventions. It was too much of course for one day, but even when it was time to leave we did so with great reluctance, looking back as if we had been in a place that couldn't possibly be real.

We sat at two outdoor tables for a very simple lunch that cost Blanche Fulton twenty-five cents each. And in the late afternoon she bought each of us a Scotch scone for a nickel apiece. I looked at the two women who prepared the hot scones and served them, because I had heard that my mother worked at the Fair selling Scotch scones, but I didn't see her. It was all right, though. I was well, and having the most incredible time I had ever had.

The whole place was all great space, all light, many sounds, including the human voice, much music, and many delicious and unknown but fascinating odors.

We arrived back at the Orphanage in time for a big meat-pie dinner at our own table, and after dinner all of the big boys who had not yet been to the Fair came to ask us about it.

143

54. The Royal Hibernian Hotel, Dublin, 1939

STOPPING AT HOTELS IN THE BIG CITIES OF THE WORLD IS a joy to a new traveler, and I must not forget this, for it is one of the delights of the human experience. The hotel one stops at in a new city doesn't have to be the best in town by any means. It can even be one of the worst, but being there, in that new city, is a beautiful thing. Everything is new, everything is different, everything is ready and right. The old, shabby hotel is new to the traveler, the old furniture in his room is new to him, the old people at work in the hotel are new people, and different, and astonishing.

The Royal Hibernian is one of the best hotels in Dublin, but in 1939, when I stopped there, I did not know that. I chose the place because of its grand name. And I was accepted immediately. Nobody said, "Sorry, there are no rooms." I was escorted to my room by an old gent who carried the bags, and when I gave him a shilling he was very happy and explained about the windows and the bath and all sorts of other things that might just be helpful for me to know. The room was not the best in the hotel. It was probably even a little less than average, but I was delighted to have it, and to unpack my suitcase, and to sprawl upon the nicely made high-up bed, for the bed was in Dublin, in Ireland, and Ireland was a place of great and deep meaning to me.

And I had money, there was always plenty of money in my pockets, and I had earned the money. I had earned it by writing, not by working at some job or other that I didn't like at all. I had earned the money by doing work I liked to do, that I *had* to do, that I would have done even if I might never be paid for doing it, as in fact I had done for so long. And then I had finally broken through, in 1934, and ever afterward I had had money, I had had plenty of money, it just kept coming in, but if it began to let up I just sat down at the typewriter and worked a few days or a few weeks, and again the money began to come in. It was great, and the best way for me to enjoy the money was to spend it in travel, stopping at hotels in the different big cities of the world. But now, in July of 1939, shadows were falling over the cities, as the saying is. The worst was about to happen, and nobody knew how to prevent it from happening. Still, it was none of my doing, so I tried to forget it, and, even though I never really did, I was especially glad I was in Dublin, in the biggest city of Free Ireland.

I was soon out of the room at the Royal Hibernian, walking in the sunlight of O'Connell Street when a man came up to me and said, "You're William Saroyan, aren't you?"

It was Frank O'Connor, whom I had never met. He was with a pleasant young lady who was his wife, or was about to become his wife, and we went to a well-lighted place with tables where we drank coffee and talked. I didn't know he was one of the greatest short story writers of the world—or would soon become such a writer. I just sat there and drank coffee and listened and talked and felt great—with the shadow of disaster dispelled in my mind for a moment. Perhaps, by God, perhaps everything would straighten itself out and the world would be spared another rampage of bloody madness. We went on talking, and met later and went out to a beer-and-song party in Killiney, and then I roared through Dublin to Stepaside with Brian O'Nolan and Niall Montgomery and several others until four o'clock in the morning, when I went back to my room and fine bed at the Royal Hibernian Hotel, and remembered the hell ahead and knew nothing and nobody was going to stop it from happening.

55. The Ritz Hotel, Boston
October, 1939

FROM DUBLIN IN JULY I HAD SAILED BACK TO NEW YORK, and then I had taken a train to San Francisco, where I had written two new plays, *Sweeney in the Trees*, and *Love's Old Sweet Song*. During May of 1939 in six days I had written *The Time of Your Life* and I had put my cousin, just twenty, into the play, in a part especially written for him, so he would be sure to have a job with a weekly paycheck, and this cousin did me one of the greatest favors anybody could ever possibly have done: he wrote to me saying the production and direction of the play were absolutely magnificent. And then he said the play was being perfectly performed. And then he said even he could tell everybody connected with the play knew what he was doing. And then he said he was learning many things from these brilliant people who were so good at making something in manuscript come to life on the stage. And then he said it was his own personal opinion that the play was a great play. In short, my cousin told me in unmistakable language that the play was being murdered by a lot of arty-farty people. I phoned United Airlines and flew to New York, from whence I took a train to New Haven, arriving just in time to see the very first performance of *The Time of Your Life*.

It was unbelievable. It was stupid. It was pretentious.

It was queer. And it just wouldn't do. Everybody connected with the play knew it wouldn't do, but nobody knew what to do about it. But I did. My career as an American playwright was at stake. I told the producers I would direct the play. I told them to get rid of the director, the scene designer, and various other people. The producers were scheduled to open in Boston in three days. I told them to meet the schedule. They thought I was mad of course, but then what could they lose? The play was quite plainly a total loss. At least they would salvage a few thousand dollars by going on to Boston, and if I made matters worse, as they were afraid I would, well, they would substitute another play for their subscribers in New York. We went on to Boston and I had a suite at the Ritz Hotel. The theatre was a walk of four or five blocks, some of it across Copley Square. My cousin acted as my private secretary, ran errands, and reported scuttlebutt every evening. Room service was great at the Ritz, and next door to the theatre was a very famous fish restaurant, so that there was plenty of good eating in Boston during the fresh staging of the play.

A new set was installed on the stage. Bogus Stanislavski-style actors were fired and replaced by working actors—who looked right and moved right. The critics in Boston saw a performance after only three days of rehearsals and previews, and the producers were amazed that the critics thought so well of the play. Perhaps I *did* know what I was doing, after all.

Backstage one evening came a famous American playwright, Philip Barry, author of *Here Come the Clowns*. With tears in his eyes, he said, "You have done what all the rest of us have wanted to do but haven't been able to do."

I was deeply moved, but the play was still far from what I knew it really was and believed it would soon become.

My cousin reported the backstage news every night: "Everybody thinks you're crazy, except the girl who plays Mary L."

Next night, "The guy who plays Kit Carson thinks you're working a miracle."

Finally, he reported that everybody got the idea, even the producers. The two weeks in Boston, getting the play ready for New York, were full of backbreaking work, but they were great weeks, too.

56. The El Rancho Vegas Hotel, Las Vegas, Nevada, 1949

I HAD A LARGE ROOM IN A DETACHED COTTAGE IN WHICH there were four such rooms. I got to bed very late every morning and slept the drunken sleep of the losing gambler.

It was November and I had been sick since April, when the little woman had met the terms of a standing agreement between us that if either of us had ever lied to the other in any important way, and had confessed it, the marriage must end.

And the little bride had confessed it—she had taken six years to do so, and she had chosen the moment that suited her best. She was twenty-eight, and I was forty. She hoped I would continue in the marriage anyway, really she did, she said. Really. I understood instantly how a father might suddenly destroy his entire family and himself. I couldn't look at the woman.

I took an airplane to Europe and wandered around in a daze for three months. When I got back to New York I saw her when I went to see the kids, and she was having a grand time. But again she said she hoped I would come back—and then she said, "Really I do." I took an airplane to San Francisco, and then I went to Las Vegas, to establish residence in Nevada, and to live there the necessary six weeks in order to obtain a divorce.

In the meantime I was drinking and gambling every

150

day and all night. I made a deal for three books with a big publishing house. They sent me an advance of thirty-six thousand dollars, and the first thing I knew half of that money was gambled away. I insisted that I would win back my losses and a reasonable profit for my time and trouble, and then I would quit—drinking and gambling both. The divorce would come through, and I would go about my business. I would go back to where I had been before the War, the Army, the Marriage, the Kids, and the Little Bride.

Well, now, how can any man who is not a fool throw away life and money that way, first in a hopeless marriage, and then at hopeless gambling?

Well, from the earliest years of my life I have known that "A fool and his money are soon parted." Who is it, though, that takes the money from the fool? Well, it is other people. And with the money, these people take other things, not excepting frequently life itself. The people who take the fool's money do not appear to be fools, but they *are* fools, only of another order, and the order does something interesting to their faces, especially to their eyes, which frequently appear to be the eyes of weasels and other sleazy animals.

Every hour I spent in Las Vegas was part of a killing nightmare. It is a wonder that all I lost was $50,000.

57. Hollins Street, Baltimore, 1940

In the early Spring of 1940 I went to Baltimore for two weeks to get my third play in shape for Broadway. The name of the play was *Love's Old Sweet Song*, and the star of it was Walter Huston. We had had a week in Philadelphia, now it was Baltimore, and there was no time to lose. At first the play had been a farce-tragedy, if there is such a thing, but in Philadelphia I decided that the tragedy part of it was not right, and there didn't seem to be any way to make it right. The rest of the play, the first two acts and most of the third act, were high-spirited and full of mistakes, misconceptions, misunderstandings, lies, pretenses, dreams, ambitions, desperations, all of which revealed man simply as a helplessly comic figure, and then suddenly near the end of the play everything glommed up and people began to die—by fire, by smothering, by smoke, by asphyxiation. And it wasn't working. No matter what I did to make it work, it didn't work. And so at last, after three performances in Philadelphia, I said to myself, "The hell with it, let the thing be a comedy, let it be a farce from beginning to end."

This was very easy to achieve, and the performances immediately improved and the audiences went away from the theatre satisfied—not confused, not surprised, not unhappy. And so my work in Baltimore was mainly to watch rehearsals and to remove flaws and to enlarge or heighten values. But even this work in the staging of a play is hard work, and especially so in that in the play were eleven kids ranging in age from sixteen down to three, and of course these kids were kids, not professional adults. They were good kids, every one of them, but during every performance one or another of them forgot his lines or his business, and this was something that had to be carefully watched, so that the play might be smooth in performance by the time it reached New York. In addition to the kids there was a rather eccentric Greek I had hired in New York outside the Guild Theatre offices on 52nd Street because his accent was so amusing, and his face and manner so theatrical. But alas, he could never be made to pick up his cues, and he was quite a lot of bother in Baltimore to Walter Huston.

I went to the Greek finally and said, "If you don't pick up your cues tonight, if you don't do your work properly, on behalf of the play, the Theatre Guild is going to fire you—they've brought down a professional actor from New York to take your part. I want you to stay. So it's up to you."

And sure enough, his performance that night was so good even Walter Huston was confused.

"This man has *got* to be a professional," he said. "He couldn't have improved so quickly if he weren't. He's been giving us the business, that's all."

And the Greek continued to give perfect performances. Hence, I could relax a little.

George Jean Nathan had suggested I call on his old friend H. L. Mencken. When I phoned Mencken, he asked me to come to lunch at his house the following day.

He looked precisely as he does in his photographs. There was a wry humor in everything he said, very softly spoken, and in his presence itself. The world was a funny place, the human race was a funny race. It was as simple as that. I invited the great man to come to the Ford Theatre and see the play, but he said, "Oh, no. I never go to the theatre." And he explained at some comic length why. The following night I met him in the back room of a saloon where once a week he was joined by cronies, many of them from Johns Hopkins, and we all drank beer and talked for two or three hours. The play got bad reviews in New York, and had a very short run. But it is a good play and it will come back.

58. 1707-A Divisadero Street, San Francisco, 1929

THE PLACES THAT I HAVE EXPERIENCED AND REMEMBER from time to time but mainly forget are here and there, although quite a few are gone: 3361 Peralta Way was the official address of the Fred Finch Orphange in Oakland, or so I have come to believe. Whatever the name of the street was, it was changed to Coolidge, obviously during his administration as President. Not far off was the Sequoia School, the first school I attended. Lunch was brought to us from the Orphanage, and it was generally a bologna sandwich, or a peanut-butter sandwich, and an apple. I thought I hated the peanut-butter sandwich, but years later I realized that I had always really liked it. I certainly took all the time that was necessary to chew the dry sandwich, perhaps it was all that chewing that made me believe I disliked the sandwich. Near the Sequoia School, which was a brandnew school, there was a small grocery store, of the kind that is always near a big public school. Sometimes I used to go in there with Sammy Isaacs or Teddy Dolan or one or another of the boys in my ward, just to look at the penny candies in the glass showcase. Now and then the grocer would look at us and say, "I think I have something for you boys, in this old packing box."

And sure enough he would lift the lid of a cardboard box and hand each of us a licorice strap, or a jawbreaker, or a wax Kewpie, or one of the many other penny marvels. (And such stores are still in business, and such penny bargains are still sold to kids.) But I have never been able to forget this good grocer.

One day at Sequoia School there was quite a ceremony: a new *Sequoia* redwood tree was planted, and somebody made a speech, and all of us looked at the little green tree but saw (as the speaker asked us to do) a mighty redwood, grown up from it. He did not say that the growth would take a couple of hundred years. As a matter of fact Henry and I, about ten years after we left the Orphanage, paid an anonymous visit to the Sequoia School, and saw that it was a dismal little building, and there was no redwood tree anywhere. It had died, and nobody had cared, that's all.

There was also the furnished room on Laguna Street where I stayed for a short time with my mother, in San Francisco, on temporary loan from the Orphanage, as it were. Those few weeks I went to school in that neighborhood of San Francisco, and of course everything was different: much less organized than at the Orphanage. But I liked the freedom and the general atmosphere of haphazard order. My mother worked for a well-to-do family during the day, and so after school I had a few hours to use up, which I did with great pleasure. One day I was riding the back step of an ice-wagon when my mother came by. She hauled me off the wagon and walloped me three or four whacks. I had never seen her so excited. When she calmed down she said I might be very seriously hurt in playing that game. And that was the end of the matter. (But whenever she wasn't around I swung up onto the ice-wagon step and rode along happily. There was absolutely no danger, I felt. And of course there wasn't—except that there was.) But soon the Orphanage insisted I must go back, and so back I went—but it was all right, it was no big deal, although I went right on hating the place.

For a while after 1929, after my return from New York, the five of us in the family moved across the street from 2378 Sutter Street to 1707-A Divisadero. I worked whenever there was a job, and for $10 I bought an enormous old-fashioned baby-grand piano—sometimes I put a blanket on top of it and stretched out up there for a nap.

59. Rooming House Behind the Public Library, Los Angeles, 1926

FOR A LONG TIME THE PLACES WHERE I STAYED WERE NOT my own. They were not places I had chosen and gone to of my own free will. But I began to get to such places in July of 1926. The first such place was a kind of tool shed converted into some kind of room on Van Ness Avenue near Belmont in Fresno, which I rented for two dollars a week, but the place had a smell, and one night was all I could take. I went back to 3204 El Monte Way, and if my return was not glad, it was wise.

A few days later I hitched a ride—anywhere. And I arrived in Los Angeles and found a room in a very old building behind the brandnew Public Library. And a job at Bullock's Department Store—Delivery Department. But after three days I couldn't ignore the sickness that had seized me, so the boss of the Delivery Department sent me home. I had a high fever, the world was stupid, and life was no good. After about 48 hours I was at least able to look around and try to think. The time was midnight. I got up and shaved and took a bath and put on my clothes and went out and walked in the streets, and went back to the stinking room and back to bed. I didn't want to run home, and in any case I didn't have the money for a train or a bus ticket, and I didn't want to try to hitch back. I found a recruiting tent in a downtown park, and joined the National Guard for two weeks in Monterey at a dollar a day—but the Army was not it, either. The Army was stupid and full of little posers, many of them crooked. But at least a beginning had been made in making and occupying my own place in the world.

My next stop was San Francisco, after visiting Fresno for a couple of days, mainly to let everybody know I was on my way. I was just eighteen, and it was about time I started my career in earnest, whatever my career might turn out to be. I was a writer, but how could I be absolutely sure about such a thing when nothing I had written had appeared in print, and I had no money and no proper place in which to work? In San Francisco the places where I stayed weren't the best in the world, either, but they were the best I had seen so far. And I didn't take sick. I was O.K., and the world seemed to be not only tolerable again—it seemed to be a rather exciting place.

But the real places that I finally came to know, the places that were real because they were truly mine, by my own choice, at my own time, I did not even begin to know until I had broken through, until I had become a published writer, until I had money in my pocket, and a portable typewriter beside my suitcase, and could sit down at a table in a hotel room and write something that would be bought by a magazine editor for better money than I had ever earned at any other kind of work. In short, the places improved as I learned to work effectively at my chosen profession.

It was very simply the greatest feeling in the world for me to arrive in New York and go to a hotel and go to my room and set up my work, and to write something, and then to go out into the city and walk and look around. That was freedom, that was truth, that was reality, that was meaning.

Hotel rooms have always had great importance to me. One of the first plays I thought of writing in New York in 1928 was called *Four Rooms*. That would have been a fine play, but it got away, too.

60. The King of Kings in the Place of Places, 1969

ONE HAS HEARD OF THE KING OF KINGS. SURELY THERE is also such a thing as the Place of Places. For us, that would be the world of course, or more accurately the earth, although there are Christians and Moslems who affect a preference for another place, and a better life than the mortal life. Great promises are made by Jesus and Mohammed, or at any rate practitioners of these religions speak of the glories to come after this life and this world. Well, of course they are not altogether mistaken, even if only oblivion is the portion of each man —or The Eternal Sleep, which is also a little on the excessively grand side as an identification of the condition which follows the cessation of mortal inhalation and exhalation, so to put it. Essentially the Place of Places is not Heaven but the World. And one is here to notice, to experience, to know this simple truth. It is for all practical purposes the only place. There is no easy escape from this life and this world, although there is death, there is suicide, there are many kinds of sleep, there are narcotics, there are alcoholic beverages, as the saying is, there are many small means of small escape, but in the end it is morning, a man finds himself still housed in his body, accompanied by his mind, his spirit, his character, his identity, his sickness, and he knows he must stay at least a little longer.

It does not matter what each of us happens to think about the world. The fact is it is quite simply the body and soul of each of us. We have no other reality. The age of the earth is newly fixed every few years, and the last figure I heard was something like four hundred billion years. That is quite a portion of time, but when that amount of time is gone, or any amount of time is gone, what we have again is only now, the present, this instant, and each of us has only his own body and soul, and his own little place in the large, large old, old place. If this isn't something to rejoice in, then nothing is. To think that, out of all the time gone, one himself has finally arrived, and is here, in a place in the world, but more importantly (although not really more importantly, only equally importantly, since man and the world are inseparable) in his own body. And what a place his body is. What an unbelievably tough, muscular, enduring, fantastic place it is, all charged with billions of secret impulses, memories, longings, expectations, compulsions, fears, loves, annoyances, anxieties, absurdities, inclinations, revulsions, and so on and so forth very nearly endlessly. In each man's body are of course the bodies of all other living, moving things, from the beginning, from the one-cell form of life, to the extinct mammoth of millions of years ago.

A man is himself the Place of Places, alive in the other Place of Places, the little runt of the Universe, the Earth, with its marvelous Toy, which man himself made, the World. How strange the word is, how strange the idea is. Places, places, places connected by paths and roads and streets and highways, and finally by ships following sea lanes and by airplanes following air lanes.

How can anybody say it isn't marvelous? Very easily. Just let a tooth rot in your mouth, and let the nerve in the tooth begin to ache, and you can very easily say the whole thing isn't worth a fig. Or let other kinds of decay and destruction happen to you, in your place, and you can curse the whole magnificent, marvelous miracle.

But most of the time a man's body and soul in the world on the earth are the greatest little accidents that ever happened to him, or could possibly be imagined as having happened.

61. Bitlis, Fresno, Los Angeles, 1926

WHERE YOU ARE DROPPED, AS THE SAYING IS, IS WHO YOU are, at least in a certain limited sense. If you are dropped in Bitlis but are soon taken to New York, Bitlis is less who you are than New York is. But the place you knew first is at least a large part of who you are. Places make people. They very definitely do, almost physically. Places procreate. They are part of the human procreation process. There are many men and women who wouldn't think of engaging in the procreative act in certain places of the world, and there are other places in which nothing seems more right and pleasant. There are places that are all business, and places that are all fun and frolic, and still other places that are all light and song and the senses and love.

After the World, after being Anywhere at all, my place was Fresno, and as far as I am concerned it was the very best possible place for me to be—and for this reason: that's where I was dropped. The minute we met, that was it. We belonged to each other. Forever. It was a fact. I was born there. I wasn't born in Bitlis, Marseilles, London, New York, or anywhere else. I was born in Fresno. It was my place. I loved it. I hated it. But had I been born in Paris, I would have loved Paris, and I would have hated it. Fresno had great early appeal for me. It had a fine smell of dust, of the desert, of rocks baking in the sun, of sand with cactus growing out of it, of water flowing in rivers and ditches, of orchards and vineyards set out in great geometric patterns, of leaf and blossom and fruit. It also had all of the smells of rot, decay, and ferment: the great heaps of grape pulp and skin at the wineries sent a smell all through the town if there was a little wind stirring. There were also the magnificent smells in the house in which one did one's early time: the very walls themselves, the people who lived in the house, and the things they cooked or baked: Armenian bread, for instance, in the three popular forms prepared by the Saroyan family: the round, wafer-thin flat bread, the oval loaf bread only an inch or two thick, and the diamond-shaped little loaves of butter bread. There was also always the smell of various green things, or growing things—parsley, mint, basil, onions, bell peppers, tomatoes, cucumbers, and so on and so forth. All of these things were a part of the place, and very quickly a part of me. For instance, after I got out of the National Guard in Los Angeles in August of 1926 I was still half-sick from the sickness I had fought in the furnished room behind the brandnew Public Library. Something was wrong. I wasn't myself. Things were assaulting me from all sides, breaking me up. I wasn't in one piece.

As I was standing on a corner waiting for the cop to wave the pedestrians across the street, a car drew up and stopped, and at the wheel was my father's kid brother Mihran. I couldn't believe my eyes. I was just eighteen, he was about thirty-two, at the wheel of his old Buick, with the top down.

That evening he took me to a Greek restaurant where the food was like the food at home. I ate vegetables with lamb, and that was it—the good food with the good smell brought me back together again. And so did running unexpectedly into a member of my family. Fresno was my place, and my family was my place.

How lucky every man is in being where he is, and from the millions of years of his people, whoever they are. Well, he can be sure of one thing, if they are here at all, they've been everywhere, they've been everybody —he is himself the King of Kings.

62. House at Ventura and Eye Streets, Fresno, 1908

THE PATTERN OF RELATIONSHIPS BEGINS TO REVEAL ITSELF quite early in the life of a man: he has to notice that there is a cave quality to all places. It can't be avoided. The curves of space can be stretched to straight surfaces, but the place remains a cave, a place. From the most primitive to the most worldly, the human being finds a place to rest somewhere, ready-made, or he makes such a place, and it is *inside,* it has limits, and it keeps out the things the human being doesn't want or the things he fears. In this place he can catch his breath, he does not need to be forever turning to see if anything is about to attack him, he rests, he relaxes, he exhales deeply, a long sigh of relief, and he eats something and he drinks something, and he remembers and thinks, and he sleeps, and in his sleep it is all there again, what happened just lately, what happened long ago, and the shape of the place of his sleep is the same as the shape of his living—it is a cave, sometimes very small, sometimes as large as anything ever is. The tent is the same as the castle. It is all in, away, safe, with clearly defined limits which declare, "This place is taken, it is mine."

For the brandnew life, without memory, or at any rate without that stage of development in memory which permits the new man to actually recall specific parts of his actual experience—places, people, voices, words, smells, sounds, and the various flavors of things consumed—for this new man the earliest hours and days and years of his experience are helpless: he finds himself carted about, held, moved, washed, fed, clothed, spoken to, and otherwise attended. Everything has the shape of the womb, from whence he so recently came. He is kept in, close to his source, held firmly to the exterior of that body, fondled, embraced, and made to know that he is somebody somewhere. That is, here, in this circle of kinship—of intelligence and love.

As memory begins to find itself real, something slightly different from experience itself, the new man notices places and people. And finally, when he is able to speak and walk and has begun to speculate about the probability of who he is, he finds himself in his own room, or in his own corner of a room. Thus, "This is me, and this is my place." And of course each place goes right on being a variation of what he knew from the beginning, a variation of where he had been before he was fully himself, and out, and began to be noticed and cared for.

And then as time goes by, whether he actually goes to school or learns what he needs to know by other more direct means, he begins to notice his head—its exterior shape, roundish, with something inside there, back of the eyes, the nose, the mouth, and between the ears. There is something back there. It is of course himself, or his family, or the human family, and it is in that round place, and it will stay there as long as he himself stays anywhere. Inside the roundness of his skull there is this person, this part of all persons, and it seems to be

himself, but at the same time it seems also to be another person, another thing, somebody else, something else. But whatever it is, it belongs to him alone.

And finally he notices the shape of the earth, of fields, of the sea, and he notices the sun and the moon, and it is all round, going around and around.

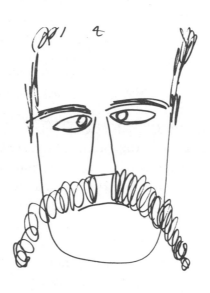

63. The First Armenian
Presbyterian Church, Fresno, 1919

REVEREND M. J. KNADJIAN WAS THE PREACHER, AND I sometimes rather liked accepting the instructions of my mother to stay for Church after Sunday School, because the tall gentleman in the cutaway coat spoke both English and Armenian, had a good voice, and now and then told an interesting story. He had married an English-woman, as so many of the graduates of the American Missionary Schools in Armenia had done, and he had half a dozen boys and girls, but I don't remember having seen any of them, certainly not frequently enough to have something to remember about them. But I did hear their names spoken frequently—rather English names. Knadjian himself was all-out Armenian, although he spoke a crisp, almost classic English, with just a touch of dry, brittle style or accent, which made his English seem authentic and mine (for instance) haphazard. Perhaps the reason I didn't see his kids was that they were much older than me, or perhaps their mother marched them off every Sunday to another Church. Who knows about such things? Or perhaps I saw them, again and again, but didn't know who they were. There is a lot of that, of course.

170   Several years ago I saw a For Sale sign outside the Church, and the price was around $18,000. I was about to buy the Place when a stock-and-bond broker explained that any investment must earn at least eight per

cent interest if it is not to be considered a poor investment. I bought a lot of hot stocks from this clever young
man, and he kept telling me from day to day how much
the money I had invested had earned. I had turned over
to him $100,000, and in about a month he claimed that
this money had earned eight thousand dollars. In the
end I lost about half of the money, and his broker-
age house kept writing to say that I owed them money
—they had overpaid me. I had to turn the matter over
to a lawyer. All because the Financial Boy felt that in
buying the old First Armenian Presbyterian Church I
was making an unsound investment—or rather in thinking of buying it. The fact is that something else pre-
vented me from going through with the purchase. I was
afraid to buy it. The place was deeply centered in my
memory. I could actually go and buy and own such a
place, but it would be a profound interference of some
kind.

When I sat upstairs to listen to Reverend Knadjian's
sermon and looked down at the benches, every place
taken, I imagined that there were a great many people
there, a multitude, in short. The fact is that the Church
could scarcely contain two hundred people. The balcony ran around the auditorium. There were two rows
of benches on the sides, and four at the back of the
balcony. Still, I had always imagined that a great multitude was inside the Church.

After he had been retired for many years, and I had
had three or four books published, Reverend Knadjian
came to the house at 1821 15th Avenue in San Francisco
one day when I was in New York and he left for me an
inscribed copy of one of his ten or eleven books—historical, patriotic, poetic, religious. This particular book
was patriotic: I found it absolutely fascinating—well-
written and with great dignity.

64. Fresno High School, 1922

"PLEASE STOP DREAMING," A TEACHER AT EMERSON
School once said to me, and I replied, "I am not dreaming, I am thinking."

But the teachers continued to ask me not to sleep in
class, until at Fresno High School I actually sat at my
desk and frequently fell asleep, sitting up. This was the
consequence of working the night shift at the Postal
Telegraph Company, from four in the afternoon until
midnight. At fourteen a man somehow needs more than
four or five hours of sleep a night, and that was all I
got for quite a few months. I tried to sleep at school in
a way that would not attract attention, but frequently
a friend across the aisle would have to push my shoulder,
so I'd wake up quickly and notice that I was drooling.
It was very embarrassing of course, but there was nothing
for it, I needed sleep badly around two every afternoon.
After about an hour of intense need, whether I got in a
few winks or not, I was O.K. again, and I would be wide
awake the rest of the day and until bedtime around one
in the morning. Still, I wouldn't have given up my job
at the telegraph office for all the sleep in the world. The
job had the first importance in my life. It was everything
to me. And I took pride in being the best messenger at
the office, and in knowing all of the work at the office,
excepting how to send and receive telegrams—or in short
to talk and listen to the Morse Code of dots and dashes.

I have always been slow (or even backward) about learning such things, and I consider it a great triumph that I learned Touch Typing, as it is called—for that ability has saved me much time, and spared my eyes.

But sleep *is* a place. It is both a simple and a mysterious place. It is where a good amount of the private or personal experience is lodged and recorded, as well as an even greater amount of family, race, group, or collective experience is stored. When a man goes to sleep, he *does* go—it is a departure and an arrival. The traveler is a traveler: it is not a figure of speech. He puts his immediate person away, knowing it will be there when he comes back, and he goes somewhere. He cannot choose his destination, or the quality of the place, or the people who will be there. He goes to a school, or to a family council, or to a pastoral walk, or to an assembly of people of the world concerned about war or peace, or to a rendezvous, as the saying is, with an unknown woman, totally charming and open about herself, or he goes to a private fight, or to a national involvement in war, or to a concert of songs, or to the inspired playing of the piano, the making of music never before heard, unwritten but unmistakably miraculous and majestic. The sleep of playing the piano began for me quite early, and as soon as I woke up I ran to the piano to see if it might just be true—that the inability to play had been lifted from me, and I could now express everything I knew and felt and experienced, I could do it by simply sitting at the piano and playing. But when I reached the real piano and tried to play, it was again only noise, and I wondered why it should be so natural in sleep but awake so unnatural, so much a matter of learning.

Death is called the Great Sleep. It is a good idea. But

it is probably Life that is the Great Sleep. There is not yet any mortal way to know what Death is. Other than what it *seems* to be, that is. Sleep is a living thing. It has no connection at all with non-being.

65. The St. Francis Hospital, San Francisco, 1935

WHEN I RETURNED TO SAN FRANCISCO FROM MY FIRST visit to Russia and Armenia, I brought with me an appendix that became infected in Tiflis, Georgia. Well, of course one really never knows about such things—where and when, or why, or how, and so on. In any event, it was in Tiflis that I took quite sick one night after a meal of spoiled food. I got over this sickness, or enough over it to continue my travels, and to return to London, New York, and San Francisco—without any help from the medical profession. One gets over all manner of illnesses and conditions all of one's life. The doctor is frequently as ignorant as the man with the symptoms, and the doctor can make a guess about the whole man and the specific complaint, but he can also sometimes decide it is better not to make a guess—which is what the man himself decides, until he knows something very definitely dangerous and likely to be final is wrong.

A burst appendix brought on the peritonitis that killed my father in San Jose, California, in July of the year 1911, when he was thirty-six years old. My father got over his illnesses as a rule, as all of us do. But this time he didn't. And by the time he knew he was dying, it was too late—the game was over.

I was luckier. Instead of the condition going from

175

bad to death, it only went from bad to worse, and I knew unmistakably that this was now nothing I could permit time and a little hot water to heal. And so I took a taxi to the St. Francis Hospital in San Francisco. The doctor who was looking after the members of my family was notified: Dr. Harold Fraser, who was also the doctor for James Rolph, who had been the Mayor of San Francisco and had become the Governor of California. All of this happened quite early in the morning. That is to say, I knew at three o'clock that I was in trouble— far-out trouble, that is. I got up and shaved, hoping the trouble would go away, but it didn't. For my father it did—that is to say, the infected appendix burst, and he imagined his relief was the consequence of an improvement in his condition, rather than a killing accident. In short, he was tricked, and rested in a false sense of well-being, at last. With me, twenty-four years after my father's death, the condition became even more painful. I took a bath, got into my best clothes, phoned for a taxi, and arrived at the hospital before daybreak of a very dreary day in October. Dr. Fraser came by after about an hour, and after studying the information gathered for him by the intern and the nurse, moved directly to surgery. At eleven or so, when I came out of the ether, it was all over. I had traveled far and wide and deep in the ether sleep, so that when I finally reached the destination I was trying for all the time, wakefulness, I had the sense of having been in the land of Death, so to put it, among the long, long dead, where I might have traveled forever. Hence, my being back in the world, in the land of life, affected me in a way that nothing before or since has affected me. I felt that I was experiencing the event of birth, excepting that it was into a fully grown body and into a life of much personal reality, many

176

events, much failure and much achievement. If ever I felt that a calling out of glory hallelujah made sense, it was the first minute or two after my return to myself and to the world. My gratitude was so great, breathing was like praying. My gladness was so great it was unspeakable. I never have again known the humility I then knew. It *was* humility. It was not something else. Life, personal life, human life, my own life, was a miracle involving billions of years of failure and achievement. For God's sake, cry hosanna.

66. Flower Shop, Geary Street, San Francisco, 1930

ONE HAS ONE'S CHAIR, OR ONE'S FAVORITE CHAIR, AND I had mine. It was one of six cane chairs bought in 1911 by my father, three or four months before he died. And when I learned that these chairs were the last purchase by my father I made up my mind to have them, always. But when at last the time came to put the chairs into my own house, in Fresno, there were only three, and part of a fourth. The three were taken to a carpenter, who took off the layers of paint and sanded them to their original wood finish, and then I took them to one of the few rattan workers in San Francisco, and he put back the original rattan seats, and the three chairs were installed where I could see them as they had been in the first place.

For years my favorite chair had been at the far end of the breakfast table at 348 Carl Street in San Francisco, and it was understood that it was my chair, and that the far end was my place at the table.

One morning I went to the kitchen, and in my chair was seated my mother's brother's son Chesley, so I said, "Take another chair, that's mine." He refused, and there was a dispute, but finally he took another chair, and I sat down in my place, on my chair.

I was twenty-four years old and he was fourteen. I thought he was very stupid not to understand that the place was mine and the chair was mine, and that it would not do for him to remain in the place on the chair in my presence. If I were out of the house, he was welcome to both, of course. He was a good boy, but had an odd mind and spirit—by turns kindly and mean.

I made a lift-top desk at Manual Training at Longfellow Junior High School, and it was stained from a very light cheap pine to a deep mahogany color, in accordance with the instructions of the Manual Training professor, so to call him, and the desk is still around somewhere—in the garage in San Francisco as a matter of fact, but I have never considered it really something of mine. I own up to having made it, but the thing itself is otherwise meaningless to me. First, the slanting lift top is not anything I am able to use when I am at a desk or table, it must be a straight top, it must be level. Second, the whole piece is rickety, as it was from the day it was made and finished. But I do have a table which I consider mine—from the beginning—and this table is one of the places of importance to me.

One year my father's kid brother Mihran came to San Francisco and opened a makeshift flower shop on Geary Street, and I went to work with him. One of the things we needed was a table, at which to work with the flowers brought from the wholesale market, so I went up to McAllister Street and found a very sturdy oak table, for which I paid perhaps four dollars. The flower business lasted until Easter, about six weeks, and that left us with the table, so I had it sent out to 348 Carl Street, and it was installed in the small front room where I spent my time writing. The table has served me well these many years—almost forty. I have written many works at the table, including, perhaps most important of all, the stories in my first book.

I had a pipe bed that I liked very much, although I am not sure it could be called a pipe bed. At any rate it was a bed with a Head and a Foot, and then the other old-fashioned metal parts and a spring on which a mattress was placed. The Head and Foot were of iron, not pipes, and they were designed in a decorative manner. Such beds were common, and I liked mine, but after we moved from 2226 San Benito Avenue it got lost in the shuffle, and hasn't been seen since.

67. 74 Rue Taitbout, Paris, 1969

WHAT IT IS, IS THE WORLD AND ME, AND THAT'S WHAT it is with everybody. That's what it has always been. That's all it can ever be. The world is a marvel of invention and engineering, and of many other things. The Earth is a miracle beyond the range of man's knowledge. But the guessing about it, about its connection with the limitlessly vast Universe must go on and on. And every living man, every human being, if not in fact every animal, is a simple demonstration of the endlessness of the beautiful marvel of matter in motion, of energy, of light, of heat, of the displacement of space by the great bodies in the known and unknown Universe.

Thus, the Place is everywhere. And the Person is himself—that is, Yourself, and Myself.

It is a Thing to rejoice in. I rejoice in it.

68. The Champs-Élysées, Paris, 1969

BUT THE UNIVERSE IS TOO LARGE TO BE NAMED ONE OF the places which is experienced, although this is actually true, and so it is in order to make it a smaller circle of a place. A continent, a nation, a state, a valley, a city, a neighborhood, a street, a house, and so on.

Well, it can't be done—that's what it comes to—it can't be done. The Great Place, the Only Place, is All Reality, and after that there are only favorite places.

For me they are various cities, their streets, and the places in which their people spend their time. Fresno, San Francisco, New York, London, Paris, Dublin, Moscow, and so on.

I used to like movie theatres, especially up to about the age of twenty-eight. And I used to like the theatre, where plays were performed on the stage, but that also has become something neither enjoyed nor needed.

Best of all, best of all is a long street in a city, and myself upon it walking at my leisure to see what's there.